PATRIARCHS AND PROPHETS

PATRIARCHS AND PROPHETS

STANLEY BRICE FROST

Montreal
MCGILL UNIVERSITY PRESS
1963

In many and various ways
God spoke of old to our fathers . . .

The Epistle to the Hebrews

Prefatory Note

The nature and genesis of this book being set out in a Prologue and Epilogue, it is necessary here only to make acknowledgements. The biblical quotations are with permission normally taken from the Revised Standard Version except that the Divine Name 'Yahweh' has been restored in the place of 'the LORD'. It is now well known that 'Jehovah,' is a quite wrong attempt at the Name, consisting as it does of the consonants of one word and the vowels of another. But the instinct which prompted its use was quite right: we lose a very great deal in substituting the vague title 'the LORD' for the very definite and personal Name. Other variations from RSV have been noted where they occur.

It will be recognized by those familiar with Old Testament studies that my borrowings from others are many, but since my purpose was to assume the modern critical view of the Old Testament and go on from there, I have not burdened these sketches with bibliographical footnotes.* Those in the know will recognize the extent of my indebtedness unaided, and other readers will only be distracted. But in order that my

---

* I have not hesitated, however, to refer the reader on occasion to the wealth of excellent comparative material available in *Ancient Near Eastern Texts Relating to the Old Testament*, ed. James Pritchard (Princeton University Press, second edition, 1955), cited as *ANET*.

gratitude to all those whose work I have laid under contribution might find expression, I have inscribed this small book to one who is himself not only an outstanding Old Testament scholar, but also a true preacher of the word of God.

STANLEY BRICE FROST

The Faculty of Divinity
McGill University

NORMAN HENRY SNAITH

סופר ומורה
וקהלת

Contents

PROLOGUE

The story of the evolution of the Bible, from its beginnings in tribal tradition and priestly case law down to the determination of the Canon at Jamnia in the first century and at Rome in the fourth (or even Trent in the sixteenth), is from the purely humanistic standpoint, one of the most fascinating in all history. For those who accept the scriptures as the Word of God, it is more—it is a providential history, rivalled in significance only by the providential history of the Church itself.

Even while it was still being gathered, this collection of writings began to play a dominating rôle in the life of the Church, both Old Israel and New; but once gathered and canonized, the Bible was accorded an authority which was not to be challenged for almost two thousand years. The precise definition of that authority has always eluded the scholars of the Church, from New Testament times until our own day.[1] But of the reality of that authority, the Church has never been in any doubt, from the discovery of the 'Book of the Law' in 621 B.C. until our own day.

If we cannot precisely define, we can at least describe this authority, and in doing so we find that it has been operative in three main areas. First, scripture gave to the Church its classical past. That is, it not

[1] Paul himself has an ambivalent attitude to the Old Testament; and the early development of rival Antiochene and Alexandrian schools of biblical exegesis, Augustine's discussion of the Seven Rules of Interpretation, and the medieval 'Four Senses of Scripture' are but a few of the many attempts to grapple with the problems arising out of the failure to achieve a clear definition of scriptural authority.

only established norms and standards, but it also depicted a Golden Age, to which all Christians looked back as presenting Christian institutions, habits and customs in their pristine purity. Scripture was the source of the Church's self-awareness, the mirror in which she conceived that she saw her own true reflection. Scripture also provided a common source of metaphors, images and allusions, and a common meeting-ground for well-read Christians of every communion, denomination and sect. It provided Christendom with its heroes and heroines, its tragic characters and its symbolic figures—prudent Joseph, patient Job, courageous Daniel, wicked Jezebel, impetuous Peter, doubting Thomas. These and many more became the stock types of Christian moral judgment. Like most such judgments these estimates were often wide of the mark historically, but nevertheless this was the use which the ecumenical church made of them; and she was able so to use them because the Bible was her classical literature, just as the poems of Homer were the classical literature of the ecumenical Greek world.

Secondly, the Bible was a theological authority. All doctrine had to have biblical support, and indeed at times scripture was degraded, to use a famous phrase, to the level of 'an armoury of proof-texts'. The Protestant form of Christianity has enunciated more clearly than either the Orthodox or the Roman the principle that 'Holy Scripture containeth all things necessary to salvation', and that 'what so ever is not read therein, nor may be proved thereby, is not to be required of any man',[2] but in practice the Orthodox and the Roman communions have very largely observed the

[2] 'The Articles of Religion' of the Anglican Communion, Art. VI.

4

same rule. Any doctrine promulgated must be shown to have at least some biblical warrant. For the Christian Church as a whole, the Bible has been the one universally recognized source of theological authority.

Thirdly, the Bible has been the authoritative source of piety. The Council of Nicea urged in 325 that all Christians should make themselves familiar with the Scripture, and even the Council of Toulouse in 1229 (which was the first ecclesiastical assembly actually to go on record as forbidding the Bible to the laity) made an exception if 'perchance any should wish from devotion to have a psalter, or a breviary for the divine office'. The Church of Rome has always sought by preaching, liturgy, and visual expression to communicate the content of scripture to the laity, but it has been distinctively in the Protestant Church that the reading of the Bible has been the great means of grace.

> 'When quiet in my house I sit
> Thy book be my companion still,
> My joy thy sayings to repeat,
> Talk o'er the records of thy will,
> And search the oracles divine
> Till every heart-felt word be mine.'

So writes Charles Wesley, and Mary Lathbury prays:

> 'Break thou the bread of life,
> O Lord, to me,
> As thou didst break the loaves
> Beside the sea:
> Show me the truth concealed
> Within thy word,
> And in thy Book revealed
> I see the Lord.'

B

In their biblical allusion[3] and in their scriptural piety, these two hymn writers speak for the whole of Protestant Christianity. The Bible possessed an authority accorded to no other classic of devotion, because in no other writing did God speak to the waiting heart as He did through this book. It was 'the good Book' or simply 'the Books', *ta biblia*, from whence arose its name.

It is important to recognize that this third area, so far from being supernumerary or negligible, was the primary one from which the other two derived. It was because the Bible spoke convincingly to the heart and mind of the individual and of the community, conveying, interpreting, and applying the facts of revelation-history, that the Church accepted this literature as its classic and as its authority. Devotion gave rise to doctrine, not vice versa. The scriptures were indeed written 'from faith to faith', and it was because of this ability to speak with religious vitality to the religious heart that they came to be accorded by Church councils, theologians, and private believers alike the preeminent authority they exercised for so long.

In our own day, however, this authority has been seriously challenged. The spread of education has meant that more Christians have more desire and more opportunity to read other books, and therefore the typical Christian is not, nor probably ever can again be, what one of the most deeply cultured eighteenth-century religious leaders could describe himself to be: *homo unius libri*, 'a man of one book, and that book the Bible'. The Bible may still be regarded as the great Christian classic, but Christians are no longer easily familiar with it. The scriptures are no longer the source

---

[3] Wesley is alluding to Deut. 6: 6–9; Miss Lathbury to Mark 6: 30–44.

of those phrases, allusions, analogies, and citations which together made up that quite remarkable phenomenon, the Christian idiom or dialect familiarly known as 'the language of Canaan'. Then again, literary criticism and the fierce light of archaeology have stripped away the pious idealizations, and the biblical period can therefore never again be the 'Golden Age' it once was. Even as an authoritative norm for doctrinal statements the Bible has lost its former sovereignty. The Roman Church has recently for the first time in history defined as an article of faith a dogma (that of the Assumption of the Blessed Virgin Mary) for which she has produced practically no scriptural warrant—a grave and significant step.[4] Many Protestant Churches in the discussion of Christian doctrine now allow themselves to differ on occasion from the clear teaching of Scripture.[5] It is no longer sufficient in theological discussion to elucidate the biblical teaching on a question—today's theologian must go on either to justify that teaching, or to show cause why he would modify it.

It is doubtful indeed whether, in the world into which we are now being rocketed, the Bible will ever regain its ancient prestige. Despite the rearguard actions of the neo-orthodox theologians, the Bible has already

[4] 'The Bull *Munificentissimus Deus*, containing the definition of the dogma of the Assumption, is an important document in the dogmatic development of Catholicism in that it marks a new and accentuated departure from the accustomed traditionalism of Catholic theology. The Biblical and patristic proof of the dogma of the Assumption that is contained in the Bull is extremely weak; one could even say that nothing is done to conceal this weakness, as though it were considered to be of no importance.' Giovanni Miegge, *The Virgin Mary* (London and Toronto, 1955), pp. 103–4.

[5] 'And we believe this departure from explicit teachings of the New Testament is warranted, or rather, necessitated, by the supreme teaching of the Bible that God is love. . . .' *Life and Death, A Study of the Christian Hope*, ed. by A. G. Reynolds for the Committee on Christian Faith of the United Church of Canada, 1959, p. 7. The Executive of the General Council of the United Church gave 'general approval' to the book, May 1959.

become for the ecumenical church but one among several authorities, including history, philosophy, science, and the comparative study of religion. Nevertheless, we are in grave danger of losing far more of the Bible than we ought. The time has not come—and I personally think it never will—for the Bible, not even the Old Testament, to be handed over to the historians of religion as of interest to them only. The Christian Church, for the sake of unity, and for the sake of its self-awareness, needs still to recognize in the Bible its classic literature. Moreover, it certainly needs to conserve the recognition of biblical teaching as delineating the norms and ideals of Christian doctrine. Scripture may no longer be an unquestionable authority, but it is most certainly a very respectable authority, which should not readily be set aside.

But—and this is the major point which I am seeking to make, and which motivates the publication of this book—there can be no rehabilitation of the Bible as the classic literature of the Christian Church, nor any fresh recognition of its doctrinal significance, until we seriously turn our minds to the rediscovery of the Bible as a book of devotion. This is, and always has been, the secret of the hold of the Bible on the mind of the Church, and no amount of literary criticism or archaeological confirmation or theological pontificating will restore the Bible to its proper place in the esteem of the Church unless we can first find some way whereby the scripture may again be allowed to speak 'from faith to faith'. This means that those of us who are familiar with the far-reaching implications of biblical criticism should attempt to take full recognition of the scholarly view of the text, and then try to see what this newly lighted passage has to say as religious scripture to religious men. Only as we rehabilitate the Bible as a book of devotion can its authority continue in any area whatsoever.

For some years I have been interested in this problem and have tried to approach it along a number of lines and at various levels, both of scholarship and of religion.[6] It has been my experience that it is easier to come to terms with that biblical literature which is itself the product of inner experience—for example, the Psalms or Proverbs or even the prophetic canon—than it is to deal honestly and yet productively with the historical and narrative sections. Now that so much of the Old Testament narrative is classified as myth, and a great deal more as legend, and even what is left is hardly admitted as history because of its strongly biased standpoint, how can we honestly derive any sense of the Word of God from it?

In order that I might become familiar with at least the difficulties involved, I agreed to write a series of twelve articles on Old Testament personalities for *The Preachers' Quarterly*.[7] I took each one as he came, and tried to discover what the narrative about him had to say to me, a modern, liberal-Christian student of the Old Testament. I am grateful to the Editor of that journal for permission to republish the articles in book form, for to do so affords an opportunity to look at the series as a whole, and to ask whether there are any conclusions which may usefully be drawn from

[6] Cf. *Daily Bible Studies*, International Bible Reading Association (1959); *The Beginning of the Promise*, Eight Lectures on Genesis (S.P.C.K., London, 1960); 'Israel's Wisdom Literature', *The Preacher's Handbook*, No. 7 (Epworth, London, 1961); *Canadian Journal of Theology*, Vol. V, No. 1 (January 1959), 'The Christian Interpretation of the Psalms'; Vol. VI, No. 2 (April 1960), 'Psalm 139: An Exposition'; Vol. VII, No. 3 (July 1961), 'Psalm 118: An Exposition'.
[7] *The Preachers' Quarterly* (Epworth, London, ed. J. Alan Kay), Vol. 4, December, 1958 to Vol. 7, No. 3, September, 1961.

it. There is therefore an epilogue following the fourteen[8] chapters of this book in which an attempt is made to draw out certain inferences which seem to me to have a bearing on the problem, and possibly to make some small contribution to its consideration.

[8] The study of Samson was written later, especially to conform to the pattern adopted for the book, and the last of the studies was added in order to end the series at one of the major stopping places of the Old Testament.

ABRAHAM

Now Yahweh said to Abram: 'Go from your country and your kindred and your father's house to the land that I will show you. And I will make of you a great nation, and I will bless you, and make your name great, so that you will be a blessing.' And he believed Yahweh; and he reckoned it to him as righteousness.

In the biblical tradition, Abraham has a place all his own. He has always been regarded, both in scripture and in the Hebrew-Christian-Islamic tradition which springs out of scripture, as the pioneer of faith in God. It has always been recognized that there were earlier shadowy figures before him—Noah, Enoch, Adam, for example—but the Flood cut their age off from ours. In this postdiluvian age, it was by Abraham that the real foundations of Hebrew and therefore Christian religion were laid. He strode across the empty plains of an as yet sparsely populated world, the pioneer of civilization as well as of religion. Now, however, we know that in fact there never was the total break in the evolution of civilization which the Flood seemed to represent. The Flood is a theological fact rather than an historical one. The story of civilization has been taken back by Miss Kenyon at Jericho to perhaps 7000 B.C., whereas Abraham is to be dated perhaps 1500 B.C. So, far from trekking through an empty world, he wandered in a relatively crowded, confined area in which great imperial powers had fought for a thousand years. Egyptians, Sumerians, Akkadians, Amorites, Hittites, Hurrians and many other people had organized and fought, colonized and built, traded and negotiated, and in a thousand cities had carried on the busy teeming life of the narrow Fertile Crescent which stretched from Babylonia round to the Sudan. So far from being a pioneer, Abraham came rather late upon the scene. Ur, from whence

Abraham's family is said to have migrated, was a city at least as old in his day as Rome is in ours. If while he was in Egypt he saw the pyramids, he gazed on them as the enigmatic monuments of an ancient past. Moreover, beyond the distant boundaries of history, now lie the vast plains of prehistory. The cave-paintings at Lascaux, for example, may be around twenty thousand years old. The latest discoveries relating to our human ancestors are dated at twelve million years ago. Abraham is, in fact, a modern.

In view of this, we cannot help asking what God was doing, then, until Abraham's day? Here it is that Adam, Methusalah, Enoch, Lamech and the rest have a real point. The Bible does not say that all things religious began with Abraham. It points to a long if shadowy development prior to his day, and we can now not only see that it was indeed so, but also recognize that in the neolithic settlements of Palestine in the eighth millennium before Christ or even in the more distant Aurignacian period in Europe and elsewhere, the Spirit of God was already at work in the hearts and cultures of those far-off times. As long as man has been man, God has been seeking his reverence and fellowship.

But if Abraham was not the beginning, he was a milestone, and a very important one at that. The story of man's progress—and with all its question-marks I do not shirk the term—has been one of gathering momentum. For millenia, the movement was imperceptible, but around the second millenium before Christ it became very marked in the Ancient Near East, and, despite temporary setbacks here and there, it has continued at ever-increasing pace to the present, headlong yet still accelerating speed of development today. In the story of mankind, then, Abraham stands at a strategic point. His millenium embraces the unification of Near Eastern culture, the beginnings of literature, the invention of the alphabet and the discovery of iron. Although we may push the boundary of history far back beyond him in recorded time, he still stands at the point where history began to become significant. Certainly, he stands at the point where religion becomes significant, and if the tradition speaks truly, it became significant at that point largely through his personal influence. In that sense he is still very rightly regarded as the Pioneer of Faith. Thus who Abraham was, and the kind of personality he possessed, are matters of very real interest to us all.

The bare facts of Abraham's life are very quickly told. According to later traditions, his family migrated from the plains around Ur (there is no suggestion, by the way, that they were ever inhabitants of that city) but more dependable traditions say that they came from across the Upper Euphrates, the area later called Aram-Naharaim (Aram of the Two Rivers, Euphrates and Tigris). Probably they were of Aramean stock, nomads who normally wandered round a fairly circumscribed area from one grazing-land to another. But under Abraham's leadership they left their usual haunts and wandered far south into Canaan or, as it was later called, Palestine. They even continued into Egypt, but conditions there did not suit or attract them and they returned north into Canaan. Here the valleys and fertile areas were already thickly populated and strongly held, but the little group of gipsy-folk were free to roam on the barren highlands. Part of the clan found the life too hard and the subsistence too meagre, and under the leadership of Abraham's nephew, Lot, they went down into the plains around the Salt Sea; but the decision proved a disastrous one—that part of the clan came very near to extinction. Abraham and those faithful to him continued to live the hard, austere, but free life of hill-nomads, moving from one grazing to another as necessity dictated. For a long time, Abraham had no heir other than a child by a concubine, but late in life his wife bore him a son whom he named Isaac. At an advanced age he died, leaving his son to inherit the leadership of the small clan of we might guess a hundred or so members. Thus the bare facts are not merely quickly told, but they are also remarkably unimpressive—no cities founded, no great battles won, no monuments erected, no great improvement achieved in the subsistence-level of the tribe. It is difficult to see wherein the greatness of Abraham could lie.

But nothing can be so false as the recital of bare facts. If there was nothing more to Abraham than the facts just related suggest, his name would never have survived in tradition. But there is a very great deal more, as we shall see. True, what is over and above the bare facts depends upon traditions and beliefs, but then so do the so-called 'facts' themselves. It is not so long since Abraham was by many dismissed as a solar myth, or as a father-image or a demoted godling. But we have now learnt a new respect for the patriarchal legends, especially since the evidence from Nusu became available. Nusu was a town north-east of the Tigris, ruled by a Hurrian aristocracy. There are indications, we need to note, that the earliest Hebrews had some contacts with Hurrians, or Horites as the Old Testament calls them. Those Hurrians had some curious practices with regard to family life. The marriage contract sometimes laid it down that a barren wife must herself provide her husband with a suitable concubine—one such contract requires that she be an Egyptian girl. The eldest son had a birthright as heir, but it was a marketable commodity, and one tablet records the sale of a birthright for three sheep. These and similar practices are already well known to us, because the traditions tell them of Abraham and Sarah, of Esau and Jacob. They evidently had the same social background as the Hurrians. The practices in question were as unusual to the Hebrews of the Monarchy who committed the legends to writing as they are to us, yet they nevertheless recorded them faithfully, even though in some details they were repugnant to them. For example, Abraham and Sarah were brother and sister, and therefore in a prohibited marital relationship by later standards, but the traditions did not gloss or hide that fact. This respect for facts leads us to give far more credence to the traditions than had formerly been thought proper. In his book *Aku-Aku*, Thor Heyerdahl tells how the Easter Islanders pointed to a great ditch as the 'Maginot Line' of a vanished people called the Long-Ears. Modern scientists said it was simply an old lava-channel, but when the archaeologists dug they found both were right: the Long-Ears had taken over and deepened and fortified the previously-existent natural feature. Traditions linger long among primitive people, and the stories of Abraham and the patriarchs can be accepted as tales telling of real men, not of shadowy myths or tribal projections.

Abraham, then, was a real person. But the question still remains, what was there about him to raise him up as a giant towering above his own generation and those that followed? The answer is indicated by two major facts. First, he made a number of decisions which altered the whole future of his clan. He decided that he and his people would leave Aram-Naharaim and seek a land somewhere away in the south. Inherent in this decision was a resolve and an ambition: the resolve to be homeless nomads no longer, and the ambition to become a people. As settled agriculturalists, their standard of living would undoubtedly improve, but there was something more than that: until now they had been part of the drifting, amorphous populations which swirled and eddied in the tide of events around the settled areas of the Fertile Crescent. They had no tradition, no memory of the past, no hope of the future. Their generations lived and died, and it did not matter. But from being nobodies they were now going to be somebodies. They were going to settle and become numerous. They were going to become significant.

Other men have thought and dreamed like that. It is a commonplace of socially depressed peoples that they produce such men—men like Moses and David and Spartacus of old, like Garibaldi, Parnell, Gandhi, and Kenyumatta of our own era. Patriotism is not a rare commodity. But even so short a list as this shows that it has many different forms and many different qualities. The second great fact about Abraham is that his patriotism is shot through and through by faith in God. His vision, he believes, is not of his devising, but God's. The urge to go out from Haran, the conviction of ultimate nationhood, these were not from within, but from without. The one was the Divine Call, the other the Divine Promise.

Abraham 'believed Yahweh and he reckoned it to him as righteousness'. It was not easy for him to believe in God. He lived in a crowded world, populated by many peoples, but even more thickly populated with *djinn* and demon, goddess and godling. Every well had its *'el*, every river and rock its *'elohim*, every acre its *ba'al*. But he put these all resolutely on one side. Behind all the changing manifestations of nature he sensed a Divine Being; in all the flux of events he glimpsed a Divine Purpose. He risked his all and that of his people on this one conviction and set himself to co-operate with the Divine Will, both for himself and the people his folk were to become. He reduced the whole strange and kaleidoscopic experience of life to a stark simplicity: this is God's world and in it man must seek to do God's will. This is what faith meant to Abraham, even if it meant the surrender of his own hopes in Isaac.

Abraham's greatness lay in his readiness to reduce life to this simplicity. Faith is the ability to distinguish the pattern of unity which underlies all our manifold experiences, physical, emotional, and intellectual, and to recognize that this unity arises out of a divine creative power which has made the universe what it is and daily presents us with a personal challenge. Faith recognizes that it stands daily, hourly, in the presence of the Divine and Sovereign Will. But faith is more than simply this recognition. It is also the courage which can joyfully submit in trusting obedience to the purposes of that Divine Will. It is that simplicity which can say that reverence for God is the one all-important attitude to life—or, to put it in Old Testament terms, that the fear of Yahweh is the beginning of wisdom. In these days when life seems so complicated and science is bewildering us daily with more and more wonders, we need to be reminded that it is still faith which reduces our experience to comprehensible simplicity and offers through all life's mazes a rational and sure road on which to tread.

And because Abraham believed, it was reckoned to him for righteousness. This one simple view of life brought him into a state of well-being—a right relationship with himself, with his environment, with his past and with his future, and with his God. At first, it must have seemed to Abraham and to his followers that his faith was misplaced. In his lifetime, the Promise was not fulfilled even though the Call had been obeyed. After the great trek, the Hebrews were no better off materially, perhaps rather worse off, than before it began. That is why Lot defected. Abraham 'sojourned in the land of promise, as in a foreign land, living in tents with Isaac and Jacob, heirs with him of the same promise' (Heb. 11: 9). He still remained a nomad, and even had to buy a burial lot in which to lay Sarah. But he continued to believe. Above all, he handed on his faith and his hope to his followers and descendants. Even though he died not having inherited the promise, he nevertheless died in faith and left that view of life and that way of obedience behind him as a pattern to those that came after. Because of what Abraham believed and was, Moses could arise to do his great work. Because of him, David could fan into flame Israel's belief in herself as God's People and her destiny as God's Will. Because Abraham had given this stamp and character to his people, the great prophets could discern in human history the Divine Plan and the Divine Justice. Because Abraham believed in a purposive God, Jesus could declare Himself the one who had come to fulfil that God's perfect Will. Abraham, the Pioneer of Faith, is indeed the father of us all. For like him, we too believe in God and seek to fulfil His purposes for us and all mankind.

JACOB

Then Jacob awoke from his sleep and said: 'Surely Yahweh is in this place; and I did not know it.' And he was afraid, and said: 'How awesome is this place! This is none other than the house of God, and this is the gate of heaven.'

Jacob is one of the most colourful characters in the Old Testament. What he was historically is, at this far remove, hard to determine. Around him have gathered so many legends and so many emotional forces that he now represents a rich complex of nationalistic hopes, religious ideals and shrewd psychological insights. He must, we think, have been a warm and attractive man, for in spite of all the accretions, the force of his personality still makes itself felt. Jacob remains a very human person.

Here we need to comment on this term 'legend'. In ordinary speech, 'legendary' means 'not factual', 'unhistorical', but in biblical studies we mean by 'legend' a narrative which may contain, indeed generally does contain, a considerable amount of historical fact; but it comes from the undocumented, unchronological realm of folk-tradition, wherein, for example, a story may be factually true, but not of the man to whom it is now attached, or wherein tribal history is personalized and depicted as the story of individuals, or again wherein the psychological needs of a later generation are projected into past events. Sometimes the legends simply supply plausible answers to questions which arise out of man's natural curiosity.

Thus, woven into the stories about Jacob, we find a good deal of material which provided psychological satisfactions for later generations. The incidents which show him as Rebekah's favourite son, his shrewdness in dealing with his brother Esau, his cleverness in out-witting his uncle Laban, all brought a warm glow of satisfaction to the later Israelites, for Jacob was their ancestor and Esau was the 'father' of all Edomites, and Laban the progenitor of the Arameans of Damascus. Jacob's triumphs over Esau and Laban could be interpreted as Israel's triumphs over Edom and Syria. Again, Israelites had a taboo against eating a certain sinew and curiosity asked why this should be so. The real reason had long since been forgotten, but the story of Jacob's lameness as being due to a wrestling match with an angel supplied a plausible answer. Why was a certain spot named 'Two Armies' (Mahanaim)? Because Jacob saw two angelic armies in that place. Why was another spot called 'Oak of Weeping' (Allon-bacuth)? Because that was where Jacob and his household wept for Deborah, his mother's nurse. Sometimes we can guess at the more probable reason (for example, the Oak of Weeping was probably a cult-centre for Tammuz, the dying and rising vegetation-god), but we can also recognize the psychological value of these so-called 'aetiological' legends.

But discernible within the wrappings of legend is the historical figure of Jacob. As we pointed out in our discussion of Abraham, the stories transmit faithfully a number of customs which are not characteristically Hebrew, but which we now know to be consonant with the social structure of some communities in the mid-second millennium before Christ, and this loyalty to such traditions strongly suggests that the stories have a dependable, historical kernel. Jacob is associated with the northern shrines and place-names, which suggests that he was a clan-figure of some of the northern tribes. The Hebrews of the monarchical period were a blend of many constituents, and it is clear that 'Israel' had earlier been a much more fluid concept. Some tribes or clans associated themselves with Israel, such as the Kenites, and others dissociated themselves from Israel, such as the Amalekites. Many of the tribes—for example Manasseh—were fairly clearly of mixed origin. The tradition that Jacob had two wives offered a convenient reason for historically caused groupings of clans into the Leah and the Rachel tribes, and the more lately acquired clans are further described as the descendants of Jacob's concubines. One such group had an ancestor called Israel and he and Jacob became in time assimilated to each other, so that the new figure is Jacob-Israel. Just as the family of twelve sons is probably a later rationalization to account for twelve tribes in the Israelite confederation, so too Jacob's relationship to Isaac and Abraham is possibly an attempt to bring the confused traditions of mingling tribes into order and coherence. But in all this we nevertheless discern a serious theological purpose. Abraham was the man of the Call and the Promise— the Call to venture forth in faith, and the Promise of a significant destiny if he responded. Jacob may or may not have been a lineal descendant of Abraham physically, but by this genealogical tree he and his descendants are firmly set in the tradition which flows from Abraham. It is interesting to note that Paul was holding closely to fact when he said: 'It is men of faith who are the sons of Abraham' (Gal. 3: 7), for it was indeed the Call and the Promise which constituted the Chosen People, not the people who gave occasion for their election. As Deuteronomy 7: 6–8 emphasizes, it was not because of what Israel was that she was chosen; but rather it was because certain individuals and tribes

responded to the Call and the Promise given to
Abraham that Israel came into being.

Interpreting, then, the legendary character of the
Jacob saga in this way, we can now stand back and
view the central figure. For in Jacob we are given a
full-length portrait. He is the favoured son of his
mother Rebekah, and it is not difficult to see why. She
had married Isaac at considerable personal risk, leaving her own family and people far behind, travelling
weary miles through dangerous country and throwing
in her lot with a man and family she had never met,
because she had embraced the Promise (Gen. 24:
58–60). When therefore Esau proved indifferent to the
Promise, and Jacob responsive to it, she naturally
inclined to Jacob and furthered him in his plans to
secure both the birthright and the paternal blessing.
Thus the younger son became his father's heir—and
the evidence from Nuzu shows that such a family
situation could and often did develop in the social
structures with which the earliest Hebrews were
familiar. But this success roused the hostility of easy-
going Esau, stirred for once out of his indifference, and
to escape his vengeance Jacob trekked north to visit
Rebekah's family.

So far, the only character we have seen in Jacob is
that of an eager, ambitious youth, pushing his way
ahead, careless of the concerns of others. But on the
way north a spiritual experience befalls him. At Bethel
he becomes personally aware of the being of God, and
of the providential care of God exercised through His
angels over the whole earth; and he also now realizes
that if he will take Yahweh to be his God, his personal
God and Protector, then that providential care will be
round and about him continually and redemptively.

Jacob emerges from that night at Bethel a changed man, with a new dimension in his thinking. He has a new awareness of God, a new sense of duty and obligation towards Him. But he still has a long road to travel.

The story of the night at Bethel is clearly in itself only one more aetiological legend. It answers the questions: 'Why is Bethel a holy place? How did it get its name?' No doubt the story of Jacob's experience was the shrine-story of the sanctuary at Bethel, and the rock-altar was pointed to by the priest as the very stone on which Jacob's head had rested! But someone has taken the story and given it a significant place in the unfolding development of Jacob's character—and it was someone who was aware of an experience which befalls man in many forms and which we know as 'conversion'. To become aware of the fact of God, to realize the possibility of a personal relationship with Him, to live under the shelter of His protecting love, to have a sense of loyalties and obligations towards Him—this is to rise to a new and wider plane of existence. Whoever it was who had the insight to interpret the Bethel shrine-story in this way had surely himself undergone such an experience. We call him the Yahwist,[9] since we know him by no other name; and the later Pentateuchal sources, the Elohist and the Priestly, are clearly content to follow along the line that he has laid down. But that he was a man of imaginative insight, of creative literary power, and deep inspiration, none who has studied his portrait of Jacob can for one moment doubt.

His treatment of Jacob's relationships with Laban relaxes the tension of his narrative rather after the

[9] The author of the Pentateuchal Source 'J'. He uses the Divine Name, Yahweh, freely: hence the designation.

manner of Shakespeare's scenes of comic relief. First, Laban tricks Jacob about the wedding and then Jacob scores over Laban with the speckled flocks, and then the two fence warily with Jacob gaining steadily (Gen. 31: 5–6), until he realizes that it is time to pull out of the game while his winnings are still intact. At this point, Rachel steals her father's teraphim, and the final indignity for the Syrian is that it is a woman, and his own daughter at that, who deceives and outwits him. But these Paddan-aram incidents have their own interest. Jacob is depicted as marrying two sisters, a practice repugnant to the later Hebrews (Lev. 18: 18), and Rachel is said to have stolen the teraphim, an act, the motive of which was unknown to the Hebrews and only recognized by us because we have the Nuzu material to reveal the custom that he was accounted heir who possessed the family gods. These and other evidences of veracity are built solidly into the narrative, and remind us that the Yahwist is using traditional material carefully preserved, and that its historical element is considerable. We may indeed recognize that Jacob as we now see him is the Yahwist's portrait of Jacob; but that there was a man called Jacob who lived in the patriarchal period and was one of the early ancestors of the central Hebrew tribes there is no good reason to doubt. Moreover, when we are considering the inspired character of the Bible, we need to remember that the inspiration lies often not only in the facts but also in the telling of the facts. That Jacob's career was a providential one, and that in him and through him God was working His purposes of election and of grace we may clearly recognize, but that the Yahwist was inspired to give his account of the man is equally apparent.

This inspiration rises to supreme heights when the writer comes to his treatment of the incident at the brook Jabbok. We can discern some of the materials that lay ready to his hand, and at first sight they look tawdry enough. There was a legend of a spirit which controlled the ford. Probably it took the form that whoever sought to cross by night was liable to be challenged by the demon to a wrestling match, wherein the vanquished must carry the victor across the water. If the traveller won, he was transported safely across; if he lost, the terrible weight of the river-god would cause him to lose his footing and he would be drowned in the swift-flowing current. Again, there was an old superstition that if you knew a god's name, you could compel him to do your will—the tale of Rumpel-stiltskin is an attenuated remnant of such a belief. We have already mentioned the old sinew-taboo of the Hebrew people, and the embittered relationship of Esau and Jacob. There was also the fact that Jacob had acquired another name, Israel, and that for the Hebrews a man's name is the clue to his character. Out of such materials the Yahwist was inspired to create his masterpiece.

Jacob, fearful of Esau's reception, arrives at the ford, and having sent his wives and children and servants across, remains by the ford brooding over the future. As night comes on, suddenly the spirit is upon him, and he must wrestle for his life until the dawn. But this is no ford-demon; it is Yahweh himself, forcing Jacob to confront his own past. He tricked his brother and deceived his father, he outwitted Laban and got away with the spoils, but now he must reckon with Esau. So far he had kept ahead of his past, but now his past has caught up with him. How can a man deal with his own past? How can he come to terms with his own former self? And in that long night of struggle, Jacob comes to see that this is just what a man cannot do. It is only as he abandons his own cleverness, only as he ceases to be 'Jacob', the Usurper, the one that catches by the heel (Gen. 25: 26) and overtakes and supplants his rival, and becomes 'Israel', the one who has striven with God and learnt his own weakness and surrendered his all into the hands of God, that he can learn the real name of God, and find Him to be forgiving and redeeming love. But such a wrestling and such a surrender is costly. Jacob is wrenched in the groin, and ever after limps upon his way. The old cleverness, the old self-confidence is gone, but it is replaced by a new peace of mind, a new humility, a new sense of serving not his own plans but God's austere and mighty purposes in history and for the human race. So, Jacob no longer, Israel goes forward in the morning to meet Esau with a penitence and a humility which disarms his brother's wrath.

Jacob is a figure who comes to us dimly out of the legends and traditions of Israel's undated and un-documented past. There is not the same historical definition that there is in the figure of Abraham, but in the events of his life we can see the salvation-history of God beginning to make itself felt. And in the portrait of the man as the Yahwist has set him forth, we see the face of one strangely like ourselves. For he, like us, has come into an awareness of God operative in his own life, and has learned the victory of surrender to Him. Those who win that victory learn His secret: His nature and His name is Love.[10]

[10] Cf. Wesley's hymn, 'Come, O Thou Traveller Unknown'.

JOSEPH

And he said: 'I am your brother, Joseph, whom you sold into Egypt. And now do not be distressed, or angry with yourselves, because you sold me here; for God sent me before you to preserve life. . . . You must tell my father of all my splendor in Egypt, and of all that you have seen. Make haste and bring my father down here.'

The story of Joseph will never lose its appeal. It satisfies too many desires of the childlike heart which is to be found deep-hidden in the inner consciousness of us all. To begin with, it is a first-class story. It has a well-constructed plot, it moves swiftly and with plenty of incident, it reveals the interplay of motives, it touches our emotions. In true romance-style, the insignificant is revealed as truly great, and virtue comes to a splendid triumph and lives happily ever after.

For those who want to probe into the historicity of Joseph, these many virtues are in themselves suggestive. We are strongly reminded of the innumerable folk-stories in which the penniless son of a widow, or the despised miller's boy, or even Cinderella herself, rose from obscurity to fame and fortune. There are deep psychological satisfactions in the telling of such tales. In particular, there is an Egyptian story called 'The Two Brothers' which appears to have been in circulation before the time of Joseph and which has many features in common with the Joseph story.[11] A younger brother is sadly wronged by an older brother, is sorely tempted but in vain by a seductress, wanders far from home, but finally becomes the Pharaoh and, forgiving his brother, accords him fortune and happiness, sharing with him even his royal dignity by making him Crown Prince. This is extraordinarily close to the Joseph story and has led many to think that the biblical story is, in fact, the Hebraized version of the Egyptian

[11] *ANET*, p. 23.

35

tale. Much used to be made of the authentically
Egyptian features of the Joseph narrative, its faithfulness to Egyptian customs and way of life, the genuinely
Egyptian names which it employs, and particularly
the acquaintance it reveals with Egyptian economic
history. This last refers to the way in which the crown
gained control of the land, and the peasants were reduced to the condition of serfs in a vast feudal system.
But the names in question are Egyptian names characteristic of the ninth, not of the earlier centuries, and
the knowledge of Egyptian customs is on examination
only of the vague 'local colour' variety. The Pharaoh
in question is never named, nor is the locality of his
court. The symbolism of dreams and the great part
they play in the story (Joseph, the butler, the baker
and Pharaoh all have remarkable dreams) suggest an
historical novel rather than a historical relation. On
the other hand, some Hebrews certainly moved into
Egypt and some Semites certainly rose to positions of
considerable importance. The story of Joseph is a
necessary link between the sagas of Abraham and
Jacob and the narratives of the Exodus. It seems best,
therefore, to conclude that there is a kernel of historical
fact, but that this has been worked upon by legend-
making tendencies and assimilated to the Two
Brothers theme, but in a characteristically Hebrew
fashion.

We ought to note how the Hebrew flair for charac-
terization is strongly in evidence. It was said of Jesus
that he needed no one to acquaint him with human
character 'for he himself knew what was in man'
(John 2: 25). In this, he was manifesting to a high
degree a quality of which his countrymen were remarkably possessed. Of the tellers of this tale, also, it

might be remarked that they knew what was in man. Joseph himself is a boy we have all met and suffered from—the precocious little prig, the joy of his parents' hearts and the bane of everybody else's. But despite his precocity there is genuinely good material in him, and when he has been through the mill, and has had his pride knocked out of him, and learned a mature dependence on God, he comes to a strength and nobility of character which none can fail to admire. There are such men, and when we meet with them we do not easily forget them. Moreover, Joseph is so alive and human. When he is rich and happily married, a high dignitary of the Royal Household, he uses his children's names to reflect the solidity and worth of his position—he has forgotten (Manasseh—*nashah*, to forget) his hardships and his family, he has become fruitful (Ephraim—*parah*, to be fruitful) in the land of his exile. But he is not to be allowed to forget. The seven years of famine are ahead and then his brothers will arrive to awaken old memories and to show him the real significance of his affluence—that it is not for him alone.

Or again there is Jacob. This is not the brilliant figure of the Jacob saga, eager, perceptive, vigorous, the man whose physical journey becomes his spiritual pilgrimage, and whom we last saw limping, but well content, into a serene and mellow eventide of life. This is an anxious, even bothered old man, whose sons run his life for him, however much he may resent it. 'Few and evil have been the days of the years of my life' (Gen. 47: 9), he says to Pharaoh, even when his son has been restored to him and he and his family have come into great good fortune. We have met such men. Again there are the brothers, individually not bad

D

men, but together capable of sudden impulses of great cruelty which they live ever after to regret. When the disaster befalls them in Egypt and they are arrested as spies, the memory of the old wrong rises spontaneously into their minds: 'In truth we are guilty concerning our brother, in that we saw the distress of his soul, when he besought us and we would not listen; therefore is this distress come upon us' (Gen. 42: 21). But when they are again challenged with the same decision whether to further their own welfare at a brother's cost, they refuse to save themselves by abandoning Benjamin to slavery in exile, and it is then that Judah rises to truly noble heights: 'Now, therefore, let your servant, I pray you, remain instead of the lad as a slave to my lord; and let the lad go back with his brothers' (Gen. 44: 33). It is then, too, that Joseph, assured that they are not really as cruel and mercenary as they were on that impulsive, hate-filled day so many years before, discloses himself to them as their brother ready to forgive. These are indeed men as we know them today, capable of much evil and yet also of great good. Even the lay figures in the story are convincing and credible. The butler is so very glad to have the services of the young Hebrew slave when he is in trouble, but when restored to power, he straightway forgets him, until that day when he has need of him again. There are plenty of men like him about. Pharaoh himself has but a small part in the story, but as one who, not a genius himself, nevertheless has the acumen to recognize one when he meets him, and to give him his opportunity, he plays his small part well and we are never in doubt as to his royalty. The story of Joseph is indeed a thoroughly Hebrew story in that it reveals a deep knowledge of the human heart, of its strengths and its weaknesses, the depths of its shame and the heights of its nobility.

But its significance and its place in our esteem arise from deeper considerations than these. In the Old Testament there are a number of distinct streams of teaching, each with its own pre-eminent concerns and insights. We are all familiar with the prophetic movement and its endeavour to reach and stir the conscience of the nation; and again we are acquainted with the priestly school and with its constant regard for holiness as the health of the divinely elect congregation. There is also 'the conventicle of the pious', the group in which the understanding of the innermost experiences of the human heart was constantly sought after. Yet another of these streams is that of the so-called Wisdom School. Here the desired goal is to attain to 'wisdom'—not the intellectual wisdom of the Greeks, but rather the understanding of what is the good way to live. This stream seems to have taken its rise from a particular profession, that of the scribe. As trusted, confidential clerks, as secretaries, as responsible civil servants, these men came greatly to respect those virtues which their profession more particularly demanded: honesty, dependability, prudence, patience and reverence for the settled order of things. The institutions they valued were the well-organized business or state, the well-ordered home, the well-disciplined life. Religion they esteemed very highly, for they recognized that it was both the cohesive of society and the sanction of morality. Thus they were at pains to teach not only the techniques of their own highly specialized profession, but also the well-tried, well-proven maxims of religion and morality. They made collections of such aphorisms as inculcated the good life, and we know one anthology of those collections as the Book of Proverbs. It is not in most people's estimation an exciting book, but it has, in the midst of much that is pedestrian, sayings of deep insight and moments of real beauty:

> Do not say to your neighbor: 'Go, and come again,
> > Tomorrow I will give it'—when you have it with you.
> Do not plan evil against your neighbor
> > who dwells trustingly beside you.
> Do not contend with a man for no reason,
> > when he has done you no harm.
> Do not envy a man of violence
> > and do not choose any of his ways;
> for the perverse man is an abomination to Yahweh,
> > but the upright are in his confidence.

(Prov. 3: 28–32)

We are not likely soon to forget such memorable words as:

> Happy is the man who finds wisdom,
> > And the man who gets understanding,
> for the gain from it is better than gain from silver
> > and its profit better than gold.
> She is more precious than jewels,
> > and nothing you desire can compare with her.
> Long life is in her right hand;
> > in her left hand are riches and honor.
> Her ways are ways of pleasantness,
> > and all her paths are peace.

(3: 13–17)

> Trust in Yahweh with all your heart,
> > and do not rely on your own insight,
> In all your ways acknowledge him,
> > and he will make straight your paths.

(3: 5–6)

Nevertheless, most readers find the short, pithy sentences weary them after a brief perusal, and few are attracted to stay longer either with the book, or with the rather stilted acrostics which the Wise Men contributed to the Psalter. Yet the content of their teaching is truly valuable and the virtues they inculcated are of sterling worth. Was there no other way in which their teaching might be expressed, no other presentation which would appeal more generally?

One of the more recent recognitions which the study of this particular stream in the Old Testament has brought to us is that the work of this School is not to be confined, as we tended formerly to think, to the post-exilic period. Its teachings are of very great age, and its relationships with other cultures are broad and pervasive from an early period in Israel's history. If then we find in the Joseph story just such a different and more attractive presentation of the Wisdom School teaching, there are no good grounds for arbitrarily denying the relationship because we normally think of the Wisdom Literature as belonging to the post-exilic period. And certainly, the things for which the Wise Men so earnestly contended and the virtues which they so persistently inculcated are beautifully and tellingly set forth in the story of Joseph.

Joseph rises to a high position in Pharaoh's household or, as we should say, in the Civil Service. In this office he is marked by foresight, prudence, and a zealous care for his master's business. Pharaoh himself described him as 'discreet and wise', and elevated him to a position second only to his own. But he came to be so elevated because he had been virtuous when tempted by his master's wife, and patient when falsely accused. He came to be chosen to serve in a high office because he had served considerately and wisely in a very minor one. Joseph is the prime illustration of the worth and dignity of the good servant.

He is, however, something more. The Wise Men had a great regard for family life. We see it in their words about sons and fathers and grandfathers:

> A wise son makes a glad father,
> but a foolish son is a sorrow to his mother.

> A son who gathers in summer is prudent,
> but a son who sleeps in harvest brings shame.

> Grandchildren are the crown of the aged,
> and the glory of sons is their fathers.
>
> (10: 1, 5; 17: 6)

We see it again in the great acrostic on the perfect wife and mother with which the Book of Proverbs closes. In such passages as these a deep concern for family relationships is expressed in a form which appeals to those who like aphorisms; but in the story of Joseph we have these same ideals set out in a way even a child can understand. Joseph allows his ambition to embitter his brothers and grieve his father and mother, but when he has learned wisdom he forgives his brothers and heals the broken relationships with generosity and affection. He insists that the family share in his good fortune, and although a nomad was an object of scorn and distaste to an Egyptian, this Egyptian civil servant takes his old shepherd father by the hand and brings him before Pharaoh and says with love and pride: 'This is my father'. 'Honour your father and mother', bids the Fifth Commandment (Deut. 5: 16); 'He who does violence to his father and chases away his

mother is a son who causes shame and brings re-
proach', say the Wise Men (Prov. 19: 26); but if you
want to know the kind of person a good son is, then
read the story of Joseph sending to Jacob and saying:
'God has made me lord of all Egypt; come down to
me, do not tarry' (Gen. 45: 9). The Wise Men also
taught: 'A friend loves at all times, and a brother is
born for adversity' (Prov. 17: 17), but if you want to
know the real character of brotherhood, hear Joseph
speaking to his brothers: 'Do not be distressed, or
angry with yourselves, because you sold me here; for
God sent me before you to preserve life . . . so it was
not you who sent me here, but God' (Gen. 45: 5, 8).
Where the story of Joseph is known and loved, family
life continues strong and healthy.

By this last quotation we are reminded of a further
point. In the story of Joseph there is a continual
emphasis on the providential care of God for the youth
who trusts in Him. In the desert pit, in the slave mar-
ket, in the prison and in high office, God is with Joseph
to watch over him, to guide and protect him. He is the
great illustration of that truth which was perhaps more
dear to the hearts of the Wise Men than any other:

> The steps of a man are from Yahweh,
>   and he establishes him in whose way he delights;
> though he fall, he shall not be cast headlong,
>   for Yahweh is the stay of his hand.
>
> (Ps. 37: 23–24)

In the story of Joseph the teaching of the Wisdom
School is put forward with a warmth and attractive-
ness which their polished maxims failed to achieve,
because in the story we have the truth revealed in
terms of personality and in a human situation.

Whoever the Yahwist was, he was a man of great tenacity of purpose. I think he found the Joseph story pretty well shaped and ready to hand, and how much he contributed to it himself we are not likely now to discover. But when he took it into his great Epic of the Hebrew people he did not allow it to get out of hand. He was careful to preserve the perspective of the whole. When we last see Joseph he is, as befits his Egyptian rank, embalmed and laid in a highly ornate coffin, *but not buried*. He knew, as his fellow Hebrews knew, that Egypt was not their home, and that they could not stay there. Their destiny was to be found not in Egypt but in Palestine, and that was where they would settle and become 'the Kingdom of God'. So Joseph's last words are a command that when they leave Egypt, as he is sure they will, they are to take him with them. He may have been lord of Egypt, but his home was the land that God had promised to the fathers, and he lays claim to his inheritance in that promise when he speaks his last words: 'God will visit you, and you shall carry up my bones from here' (Gen. 50: 25). In order that the links may be truly made, the Exodus narrative is careful to include the fact that Moses duly took the bones of Joseph with him. The Yahwist wants us clearly to understand that Joseph, like Jacob and Isaac and Abraham before him, was more than Egyptian prince. He was Heir of the Promise. And that was true of even the meanest Hebrew.

MOSES

So Moses returned to Yahweh, and said: 'Alas, this people have sinned a great sin; they have made for themselves gods of gold. But now, if thou wilt forgive their sin—and if not, blot me, I pray thee, out of thy book which thou hast written.'

Moses is undoubtedly the greatest figure in Old Testament tradition. He so impressed the Israelites of his own generation that he became more than a man; he became an institution. Jesus refers to the scribes 'who sit in Moses' seat' and even in his day they had sat there for many centuries.

Moses gave to Israel her most precious possession—the Law. Laws have a way of becoming out of date. There are many laws on the Statute Book at Westminster which have never been repealed but have simply lapsed into irrelevance. New times are ever presenting new situations and requiring new laws to regulate them. But so great was Moses' reputation that no one ever dared to share with him the rôle of lawmaker. As new laws were formulated, they were 'foot-noted' as it were, to his law; statutes of a day much later than his were added to the previous codes and the mass of material grew continually. In Old Testament times, the 'Law of Moses' was thus constantly expanded by the scribes; after the Pentateuchal text was fixed, the process of adapting the Law to later times was carried on by commentaries and summaries. In doing this, both the Old Testament scribes and the post-biblical rabbis were conscious of acting in the name, spirit and office of Moses. To this day, the rabbis continue to 'sit in Moses' seat'. In orthodox Jewish circles there is, for example, a carefully worked out 'Law of Moses' about the use of the telephone on the Sabbath.

Thus, more than any other Old Testament character, the life and personality of Moses is overlaid with legend and accretion. Yet perhaps the real greatness of the man is that, even so, his character shines through, and we can discern the very human figure beyond and behind the institution.

The story of his life is universally known. Born of Hebrew slaves, he was brought up in the Royal Household, being intended probably for responsible service in the Egyptian equivalent of the Civil Service. But as a young man he threw in his lot with the enslaved people and was instrumental in affecting their escape. He led them into the desert, gave them a nationality, a religion, and a law, and guided them for many years in nomadic wanderings, but died before they were successful in invading Palestine. That is the bare framework of the life, but into it was packed an immense wealth of legend, law, piety, worship, poetry, and art.

An ancient story[12] told how Sargon of Akkad, some thousand years before Moses' time, was sent adrift in a box on the Euphrates. The story was borrowed to explain how Moses grew up in Pharaoh's household. The deliverance of the slaves was made possible by some disorder which struck at Egypt (probably the death of the Heir Apparent), and this was expanded into the famous Ten Plagues. The ancient rite of the Passover, originally a moon-god feast, was adapted, possibly by Moses himself, to commemorate the Exodus, but several different ways of celebrating it are now woven together in the story of its institution

[12] *ANET*, p. 119.

48

(Ex. 12–13). How much the event shaped the later rites and how far the rites influenced the narrative of the event we can hardly determine. The institution of the covenant provided an opportunity for inserting an early law code, The Book of the Covenant (Ex. 20: 23—23: 32), but to this were prefixed the Ten Commandments, borrowed from Deuteronomy. An idealized picture of the tabernacle and of the priesthood, the regulations of the sacrificial system, the food and other taboos of the Hebrew people, but all as leavened and enlightened by the moral insights of the prophetic movement, were then inserted after the institution of the Covenant, and this complex forms the second half of our book of Exodus and the whole of Leviticus and continues into the early chapters of Numbers. Not until Numbers 10: 11 is the narrative resumed with a number of disconnected legends of Moses and Aaron, and then follow the abortive invasion of Palestine, the circumperambulation of Edom and Moab—the latter providing an opportunity for the further inclusion of the Balaam legend—and the conquest of Gilead. This brings Israel into sight of Western Palestine (Num. 36: 13), but a great deal of law and cultic regulation has been heterogeneously mixed in with the narrative. We have now reached in point of time the death of Moses, but still another great expansion intervenes. Four speeches of Moses— probably composed as a separate law-book and generally identified with the scroll found in the Temple and used as the basis of the Josianic Reformation (2 Kings 22: 8f.)—were inserted into the narrative, and these speeches were so clearly a revision of much of what had gone before that they were early called 'the Second Law', or 'Deuteronomy'. Finally, the legend of the

49

death of Moses was allowed at long last to close the narrative, but so inflated had it become that whereas Abraham, for example, has about thirteen chapters, Moses has one hundred and thirty-six. To say that Moses is an institution rather than a man is an understatement. His life was, in fact, in great danger of becoming a National Repository, a British Museum of the Hebrew people.

I have used the word 'legend' freely in describing this material. This does not mean that it is necessarily untrue. A great deal of solid history is contained in a people's legends. But it is all dateless and unverifiable, and the traditions are often modified by the motives and needs of later generations. If it were our purpose to assess the value of these four books, Exodus, Leviticus, Numbers and Deuteronomy, I should set out to show that they are to the Old Testament what the Four Gospels are to the New, and that they are of quite inestimable religious worth. I should also hope to show that they are to be received humbly and reverently as the written Word of God. Nothing that I have said detracts from this view of their central significance. Nevertheless, since our present purpose is not to estimate the worth of the Mosaic books, but rather to disinter and to reconsider the historical person, Moses ben Amram, we have to note that a great deal of the content of these books comes from later ages, and that we must reach back behind the complex of law, legend and tradition if we are to arrive at the man himself. The fact that this is in any degree possible is, as we have already observed, one of the outstanding testimonies to the greatness of the man.

A clue to the historicity of a tradition lies in its

continuing dominance in the minds of later generations. There have been many attempts to dissolve the
great figures of the past into fantasy or projection. The
name of Freud is unfortunately to be associated with
such an attempt in the case of Moses. But great men
create traditions far more often than traditions create
great men. The later regard for the Exodus event is
itself strong testimony to the overwhelming probability
that such an event did indeed take place. The un-
challenged centrality of Moses in the traditions clus-
tering around that event is weighty evidence that it
was through his instrumentality that it was achieved.
We know that at different periods Semitic individuals
and groups played a significant part in the life of
ancient Egypt, and we may freely accept the tradition
that Moses began his career as a member of Pharaoh's
'household'—a word which had the same kind of
connotation then as 'the White House' has today. The
outcome of the Exodus story largely turns on Moses'
ability to move with assurance and understanding in
his relationships with the Egyptian court in a way in
which no unlettered Hebrew slave could possibly have
done. There is also the corroborative detail that his
name is Egyptian and not Hebrew, and we recall the
tradition that when Joseph entered Pharaoh's service
he too received an Egyptian name. We may take it
then that Moses received an Egyptian upbringing and
education, and was destined for the career of an
Egyptian official.

This gives particular meaning to his espousal of the
Hebrew people and the Hebrew cause. The Epistle to
the Hebrews grasps the significance of this element in
the story when it says: 'He considered abuse suffered
for the Christ greater wealth than the treasures of

Egypt'.[13] In the famous story of Sinuhe,[14] this Egyptian nobleman had to flee the country, became a member of a desert nomadic tribe, and rose to chieftainship and honour among them. But in his old age, the call of the culture and ease of life back in civilization was too strong to be denied, and installing one of his sons in his chieftainship, he left his friends and wife and children, and made his way back to the Egypt from which he had fled. For Moses the decision was exactly the opposite. He freely chose to go out into the desert with the rabble of Hebrew slaves, and never faltered in that choice until he died. In all his endeavour on their behalf, Moses never lost sight of his original vision—that they were Israel, who were indeed not a people but should become a people, who had no place, but were to inherit the land to which Abraham had laid claim. For Moses the ideal was the real, not in the philosophic sense of Plato, but in the intensely practical sense which was to become the characteristic of his people. The ideals which he envisioned were what determined his existential choices. His course in life was consciously shaped by his beliefs, and the destiny of his people was for him infinitely more valuable, more ponderable, than all the material riches of Egypt. We may firmly believe that, like Abraham before him, Moses was characterized by his faith.

There is a further element in the narrative which strikes even the casual reader very forcibly. It is summed up in the famous verse: 'Now the man Moses was very meek, more than all men that were on the face of the earth' (Num. 12: 3). When it was believed that Moses was the author of the Mosaic books, the

[13] Heb. 11: 26; 'The Christ' may be paraphrased as 'the messianic destiny of the people of Yahweh'.
[14] *ANET*, p. 18.

52

statement was embarrassing, because if Moses wrote that, then he certainly was not meek! But now that we understand the true nature of the books, we welcome it as a comment which sums up a very remarkable element in the Moses-saga. Time and time again he is displayed as a man of humility, understanding, and patience. The traditions give a vivid picture of how the Hebrews depended on him, resented him, were disloyal to him, and how in spite of all their failings he never lost his concern for them. This is emphasized in the story of the Golden Calf, where, although his anger blazes out against them, as it inevitably did from time to time, he is nevertheless not prepared to break with them or to relinquish his efforts on their behalf. The story depicts Yahweh as having reached the limit of *his* ability to bear with them; but Moses has not done so. He can even plead that, rather than that he alone should survive and become another Abraham, God should blot him out of the book of life and let Israel go free of her fault. This greatness of heart is not likely to have been imported into the traditional picture of Moses, but must surely go back to the historical figure. He had in him something of that generosity and love which not only allows a man to be great, but also wins him the strong affection of his people. Moses lived in the traditions of his people all the more vividly because he also lived in their hearts.

Nevertheless, patriotic faith and a genuine love for his people are not in themselves sufficient to begin to explain the person and achievement of Moses. There is something more to be said. While still a young man in Egypt, Moses felt the pull of the mysterious tides of blood. He might himself be in a comfortable and assured position, but he could not ignore the fact that

E

he was one of this ill-treated and enslaved people. A sense of concern for the Hebrew slaves grew strongly enough within him to bring him to the decisive choice and to make him cast his lot with that of his own flesh and blood. But as this world of ours has yet to learn, only a patriotism which is lifted up to see the destiny of a people as part of the process of significant history —that is, of world history—can be strong enough to rise above particularism and racialism. Moses' patriotism underwent just such a transformation at the Burning Bush, in the crucible of religion.

The hallowed narrative of the third chapter of Exodus has this in common with the story of the temptations of Jesus: the subjects were humanly alone, and the account we now have is the experient's attempt to communicate to his friends something of what the experience meant to him. The resultant story is inevitably an interpretation of the event rather than a piece of factual reporting. Thus the consequent narrative is not a picture which we can look at and value for its own qualities, but rather a window through which we can catch a glimpse of the inner recesses of a soul. Moses tells of an arresting phenomenon and of the voice that spoke from its midst. How far, when he relates the experience in these terms, he is describing the actual physical facts of the incident is, then, an irrelevant question—these are the terms in which Moses conveys his experience, and we must accept them. But what we can say is that the element of the miraculous, if such an element there were, is quite secondary to the real significance of the experience. Moses became aware of Yahweh as the living God, the One who is real in life. *'Ehyeh 'asher 'ehyeh*, the familiar 'I am that I am', is probably better translated

'I cause to be what I cause to be'; that is, Yahweh is the Living God, initiating the processes of history and bringing events to birth according to His sovereign will. Moses saw that his concern for his people was not to be simply a sense of herd-identity in the face of competition from other groups and tribes, but rather it was to take its significance from the fact that their welfare was a divine concern and their destiny a divine destiny. But to say this is to recognize that Israel is not an end itself, but is being made an instrument to a larger end, indeed the total end, the whole purpose of God. It is to say 'Not our will but Thine be done'. It is to make God the Lord and Sovereign of all life. Once more, the Epistle to the Hebrews has the telling phrase: 'He endured as seeing him who is invisible' (Heb. 11: 27). That is, he was intensely religious.

Moses was a giant among men. The concepts of Law and Covenant, which modern scholarship is defending as genuinely Mosaic institutions, reveal a creative mind, such as can take over existing institutions and give them new force and significance. The stories of one who through many weary years bore patiently with an irresponsible and childlike people point to a large and generous heart. The narrative of the Burning Bush and the constant emphasis on Moses' close communion with the Lord, 'so that his face shone', remind us that we are in the presence of a saint, a true man of God. The fact that he set on his people his personal stamp which has endured recognizably through three millennia until this day, is irresistible evidence of the dynamic qualities of personality with which he was endowed. No one can deny Moses his place among the few truly great men in the history of our race. As such we can indeed admire and reverence him.

But as a man of faith, Moses is something more than a great figure of the distant past. He is a man in our situation, facing our choices, deciding the issues of our existence. Out of his faith of God, he speaks across the years to us: 'As I have chosen, so you may choose— and so you must choose.' And then he adds: 'See, I have set before you this day life and good, death and evil . . . therefore choose life, that you and your descendants may live' (Deut. 30: 15, 19).

JOSHUA

'Now therefore fear Yahweh, and serve him in sincerity, and in faithfulness; put away the gods which your fathers served beyond the River, and in Egypt, and serve Yahweh. And if you be unwilling to serve Yahweh, choose this day whom you will serve, whether the gods your fathers served in the region beyond the River; or the gods of the Amorites in whose land you dwell; but as for me and my house, we will serve Yahweh.'

Joshua is a commanding figure. We see him characteristically as standing threateningly over doomed Jericho, or with outstretched javelin decreeing the destruction of Ai, or beside the stone of witness at Shechem, summoning the whole nation to a total loyalty to Yahweh their God. He is always depicted as a man dominating every situation. Even after the defeat at Ai, he is as commanding in penitence as he was at other times in victory.

The traditions about him are straightforward and consistent. They present a continuous and unbroken front, and we can have no confidence that we can get behind them to the historical person. Whereas with Abraham, Jacob, Moses, we feel that behind the traditional presentation something of the real man still survives to be discovered, with Joshua we are left to make what we will of the official story. Joshua is in effect a public figure, and we are never granted the privilege of a private interview.

His first rôle, in which he appears rather fitfully, is as Moses' 'minister', or private chaplain. The effect, possibly the intention, is to identify him closely with the great man from the very outset of his career. The story in Exodus 24 and 32 rather suggests that Moses took Joshua up into Mount Sinai when he received the Law, though most exegetes assume that he was left at some halfway stage and picked up again during Moses' descent. Certainly he is represented as being Moses' deputy at the Tent of Meeting (Ex. 33: 11), and we also find him being nominated as Moses' successor and being carefully acquainted with certain arrangements into which Moses had entered (Ex. 17: 14; Num. 32: 28). Finally he is solemnly commissioned to be the one to lead the people into Canaan.[15] It is very noticeable, however, that he is given no title —he is neither king nor prophet, neither priest nor judge. Even Moses gets the titles 'prophet' and 'lawgiver' but Joshua has none. His rôle is simply that of Moses' successor. Almost, one might say, he is a prolongation of Moses.

We next notice him in connexion with the expedition of the twelve emissaries of Israel to spy out the land of Canaan and bring back a report. Here we notice a curious thing. In the list of the twelve, Joshua's name is missing, and the representative of Ephraim is a man called Hosea. At the end of the list we are told that Moses called Hosea 'Joshua'. Now it is true that the two names are closely related, but they are not the same, and when we find that the story is really Caleb's story (Num. 13: 30; 14: 24), we are forced to conclude that Joshua was associated with it only by later tradition. Caleb was the one man of the desert generation whom God said He would allow to enter Canaan; but Joshua also entered; therefore it was assumed that he must have been associated with Caleb's meritorious behaviour and so shared the same distinction. Joshua plays no distinctive or characteristic rôle in this incident, and we cannot use it to judge or assess the man himself; but if he was not originally involved and the story was attached to him later, this fact in itself is highly important, in that it shows the

[15] There are two accounts of this commissioning, Num. 27: 15–23 and Deut. 31: 14–15; 23.

Joshua legend to have had a strongly acquisitive character.

The best-known of Joshua's rôles is, however, the military one. It is as a soldier that he first appears in the Bible. In Exodus 17 we read that the first of Israel's battles was with Amalek, and that her forces were led on that historic occasion by Joshua, but as he is introduced without any explanation or identification, not even the familiar patronymic 'son of Nun', we may take it that when the story was inserted in the Pentateuchal narrative at that point, the Joshua tradition had already acquired its present military character. His main achievement was, of course, to lead Israel's successful invasion of Palestine, and it will be worth while briefly to review the manner of the telling of that campaign.

Joshua 1 is a deuteronomic passage of an hortatory character, and stresses the ideal unity of Israel by referring to the readiness of the two and a half tribes of Trans-Jordania to share in their brethren's military tasks. This concern with the unity of the tribes reoccurs at some length in Chapter 22, and reminds us that we are dealing with a very idealized account of events, for the Book of Judges gives us evidence of a far less co-ordinated activity by the tribes, which worked separately and in groups. The spying of Jericho occupies Chapter 2; the ceremonial crossing of Jordan, Chapters 3 and 4; and the circumcision of Israel, Chapter 5. The capture and destruction of Jericho is told at length in Chapter 6, but it is more of a religious ritual than a battle. The defeat at Ai occupies three verses in Chapter 7, and the rest of the chapter is concerned with Achan and his judgment. Chapter 8 concerns itself closely with military matters (the capture of Ai), apart from the last five verses, but it is a striking fact that it is the first to do so. Chapter 9 tells how the leaders of Israel rather than the impeccable Joshua were hoodwinked by the Gibeonites, and this leads into the story of the battle with the Canaanite coalition, which occupies a good deal of Chapter 10. The rest of this long section tells how, having smashed the central Palestinian power, Joshua moved south and conquered the southern Judean hill country, the Shephelah and the Negeb. These successes roused the fears of Jabin, King of Hazor, who organized a northern coalition, which, however, was thoroughly beaten, as Chapter 11 narrates. This is the end of Joshua's campaigning and the rest of the book is concerned with the allocation of the conquered territory to the various tribes, until Chapter 23, which together with Chapter 24 is occupied by a long hortatory passage concerned with the renewal of the covenant. It has the same deuteronomic character as the opening chapter, and is preceded by the reference in Chapter 22 to the ideal unity of Israel, as we have already remarked.

Clearly, then, the purpose of those who put the book together, and thus transmitted their version of the Joshua tradition, was not to glorify Joshua as a soldier. A soldier he certainly was, but in their view only incidentally. They gave little space to strictly military affairs. Joshua's greatest victories, the fall of Jericho and the rout of Bethhoron, are presented as divine miracles. For the rest, the deuteronomic historians—for there is little doubt as to their identity—are content to record that 'he fought against' such a town, and 'Yahweh gave it into his hand'. The account is highly stylized, and we suspect that the concept of a unified

62

campaign headed by Joshua is the product of the deuteronomists' view of what ought to have happened, rather than of a historical concern with what did happen. It is true that Dr. Yigael Yadin, now excavating Hazor, finds that it was destroyed in the late thirteenth century B.C., but whether by Joshua is another matter. Jabin, King of Hazor, is said to have been the foe of Deborah and Barak also, and they as well as Joshua are said to have destroyed him (Jud. 4: 2; 23–24). Despite Miss Kenyon's rather negative results—in this respect only—from Jericho, it is fairly certain that a wave of destruction passed over Palestine in the late thirteenth and early twelfth centuries B.C., but again this is not to prove that Joshua commanded the army or armies responsible. But the important point to grasp is that the Book of Joshua is in fact not very greatly interested in Joshua as a soldier. Rather it presents him as the extension of Moses, the one who completes Moses' work by bringing divine prophecies to fulfilment, and the one who renewed the nation's loyalty to the Mosaic covenant. It indeed describes the conquest of Palestine as due to a unified campaign, executed by all Israel with Joshua at its head, but it does this not to glorify Joshua but to emphasize that the occupation of Canaan was a divine action fulfilling the ancient promise to Abraham. The interests of the editors of the book are religious interests, and the central figure is in their view a religious figure.

What then are we to make of Joshua? Behind the commanding figure of the traditions we may suspect that there stands hidden some local chieftain, but we have no way of estimating his character or importance.

Are we therefore to dismiss the official figure as a mere valueless projection?

To do so would be to misunderstand the whole character and worth of these early biblical traditions. They come to us from over three thousand years ago, and the amount of sheer historical fact they convey is quite remarkable. There is no doubt, for example, that Israel did invade Palestine and settled there in the thirteenth to twelfth centuries B.C. and this is what the Book of Joshua bears witness to. On the other hand, we expect later considerations to have shaped the details considerably, and no reasonable person is going to complain about that. The man whose interest in these narratives is a religious one will be grateful for just this very thing. For the quality of a nation and its character are shown pre-eminently in the way it shapes and idealizes its traditions. When Israel, looking back on the invasion period, idealized Joshua and built him up into a figure representing her history as she would like it to have happened, she was pointing at those features of her history which were for her significant. Her faith was that the God of Israel was known in the things that He had done for her in history, and if she collected those things together into a single life and brought widespread instances together into a smaller compass, it was in order that she —and we who follow after—might the more easily recognize the divine activity and the more readily discern the salvation-pattern. The result may not be history as we moderns understand history, but it may be the Word of God.

The Book of Joshua is quite the most outstanding instance of this process, and this fact gives the central figure an especial significance. Other Old Testament

personalities show signs of having been influenced at
this or that point by such tendencies, but Joshua is to
all intents and purposes created by them. This fact
provides us with a very valuable opportunity. If we
want to know what the ideal servant of God looked like
as envisioned by the deuteronomic historians, we
look at their portrait of Joshua and discover the answer.
He is utterly devoted to Yahweh and intensely loyal
to the Mosaic covenant. He is divinely directed and
guided at every turn of the road. He is an adornment
to his generation, and the people respect and honour
him. As a corollary to all the foregoing, he is, it goes
without saying, successful in all he undertakes—the
defeat of Ai and the trick played by the Gibeonites
being due to other people's shortcomings, not his. He
lives to a grand old age and dies content with the
knowledge of his own integrity. Thus he is the embodiment of the deuteronomic ideal of the happy and re-
warding life. But Joshua is not only the embodiment of
that ideal; he is also the exemplar for others to copy.
The deuteronomic school was creative in the years
from the mid-seventh century into the exilic period.
This was the period when the monarchy held out its
brightest hopes in the person of Josiah, but it also held
grim memories of Manasseh and Jehoiakim and the
disastrous incompetence of Zedekiah. For some, all
this meant that the longing for a perfect king rose up
into the messianic hope; they looked for a second David
to restore their fortunes. The great passage in Isaiah
is the classic example:

> For to us a child is born,
>   to us a son is given;
> and the government will be upon his shoulder,
>   and his name will be called
> 'Wonderful Counselor, Mighty God,
>   Everlasting Father, Prince of Peace'.
> Of the increase of his government and of peace
>   there will be no end
> upon the throne of David, and over his kingdom.
>
> (Isa. 9: 6–7)

But for others, the idea of kingship had no such fascination; they were quite disillusioned on the subject. They did not at all look forward to a second David; rather, they sought a return to the good old days when every man did that which was right in his own eyes and it was right in God's sight also. In those golden days no one needed a king. It is significant that the majority of the Golden Age prophecies of the Old Testament do not envisage a Messiah. The most famous of them all, for example, has no place for the Messiah in its ideal future:

> It shall come to pass in the latter days,
>   that the mountain of the house of Yahweh
> shall be established as the highest of the mountains,
>   and shall be raised above the hills;
> and all the nations shall flow to it,
>   and many peoples shall come, and say:
> 'Come, let us go up to the mountain of Yahweh,
>   to the house of the God of Jacob;
> that he may teach us his ways
>   and that we may walk in his paths.'
> For out of Zion shall go forth the law,
>   and the word of Yahweh from Jerusalem.

He shall judge between the nations,
and shall decide for many peoples;
and they shall beat their swords into plowshares,
and their spears into pruning hooks;
nation shall not lift up sword against nation,
neither shall they learn war any more.

(Isa. 2: 2–4)

Thus, while the royalists threw their ideals into the future and hoped for the Messiah, others threw their ideals into the past and idealized Joshua. He is of the same character and quality as the messianic hope, but he is not royal, nor indeed does he fall into any type— neither prophet, priest nor king. Hence he has no title other than the simple family name 'son of Nun'. Yet he is as much an ideal as the Messiah himself. He is the great exemplar on which the deuteronomic man should mould his own life. If such a man was as single-minded as Joshua, as loyal to the Mosaic covenant and as devoted to Yahweh, he too might expect to prosper in all his affairs and finally bring his life to an end in universal esteem.

The outstanding virtue of the whole deuteronomic movement was its firm grasp on the principle of God's redemptive activity in history. The deuteronomic historians saw that activity as operating through human personalities. In the crises of Israel's life, God raised up saviours for her, and it was this view of history which led them to shape the traditions of the pre-monarchical period into the familiar pattern of the Book of Judges. Barak, Gideon, Jephthah, were the illustrations they used. They even wrestled with the Samson saga and tried to make him fit into the pattern also.[16] But the

[16] But see the next chapter. Toward David and the kingship their attitude

outstanding illustration is Joshua. Not only is he the example of the deuteronomic man, but he is also the great instance of the redemptive agent, the saviour. He led his people into Canaan, conquered the country for them, and gave them rest from their enemies round about. His very name means 'Yahweh is Salvation'.

Here then is a striking figure. It is ideal rather than historical; it is an exemplar for others to copy; it is that of an agent of the redemptive activity of God in history. It is not in the ordinary sense a messianic figure, but it does symbolize men's hopes and highest religious values.

One of the unfulfilled 'prophecies' of the Old Testament was that the Messiah's name should be Immanuel (Isa. 7: 14). We sometimes give that name to our Lord as a kind of honorific title, but it was never his name. The name chosen for him was Jesus, or, to give it its Hebrew form, Jeshua, a contraction of Jehoshua, which we normally spell as Joshua. When Joshua is referred to in the New Testament, the Greek gives his name as Jesus (Acts 7: 45). This leads us to conclude as follows. The Messiah, when he came, was the Son of David and inherited the messianic prophecies; he was also Son of Man and fulfilled the apocalyptic hope; he was in addition one who came not to be ministered unto but to minister and to give his life as a ransom for many, and thus he played the rôle of the Suffering Servant. But his personal name was Joshua, and we may think that in the divine Providence he was given that name rather than Immanuel in order that we

was ambivalent. Probably it underwent a change after the disaster at Megiddo, and the fiasco of Zerubbabel. The Book of Joshua is in its present form a later post-exilic work.

might clearly recognize that he also took up and fulfilled the deuteronomic ideal as it is expressed in the portrait of Moses' successor, who was both the Example and Saviour of his people. The figure of Joshua is for the Christian another clue to the significance of Jesus.

SAMSON

Then Samson called to Yahweh and said: 'O Lord Yahweh, remember me, I pray thee, and strengthen me, I pray thee, only this once, O God, that I may be avenged upon the Philistines for one of my two eyes.'

No one has suffered more at the hands of Old Testament critics than Samson. The Philistines tricked him, blinded him, humiliated him, but he finally turned the tables on them in a suicidal victory which left him glorious in death, inviolably triumphant over all his enemies. The critics first discredited him and then dropped him from serious discussion. For nineteen centuries Samson had been one of the Great Heroes of Christian tradition. Children were regaled with his exploits and congregations were edified by the exposition of his virtues. The divine aura attendant upon him was so unmistakable that Milton could in all sincerity depict him as noble even in self-ruin, the tragic Samson Agonistes.[17] Today he has been quietly banished from Sunday School curricula, and he is never mentioned in sermons. But he is still in the Bible. What are we to make of him?

His stories are told in that incomparable repository of Israelite tribal tradition, the Book of Judges (13: 1–16: 31). There is a nativity narrative, and there are the stories of the woman of Timnah, the woman of Gaza, and the woman of the vale of Sorek, whose name was Delilah. They are each worthy of some brief individual attention.

The nativity story tells how, at the time of the Philistine domination of Israel, a barren wife was assured by

[17] Is it too fanciful to suggest that the tragic note is inherent in the biblical as well as the Miltonian figure, in that even the final slaughter of his enemies only avenged Samson for *one* of his eyes—the other was left unavenged? Is that what the strange verse (16: 28) is meant to suggest?

'the Angel of Yahweh' that she was to bear a son, who was to be a perpetual Nazirite. Any man could take a vow to abstain from wine and any form of ritual uncleanness for a period of time as an act of devotion. During that period he was a Nazirite.[18] He shaved his head at the beginning of the period and cut his hair again at the end and offered it as a symbol of his self-devotion during the allotted period. But Samson was to be a perpetual Nazirite, and his mother was enjoined to abstain from wine from the moment of his conception. His hair was never to be cut, for his whole life was to be one of devotion. Of course, this word 'devotion' does not have the connotation of piety or quiet worshipful meditation, but rather that of 'devotee'. That he is to be a Nazirite means that he is to be fiercely, intolerantly an adherent of the Yahweh cult. It means, in fact, that he is to be a Yahweh fanatic. It is also promised that he shall begin to deliver Israel from the Philistines—a significantly vague phrase, because, in fact, he may have been a nuisance to the Philistines but he was certainly no help to his fellow Israelites. The nativity-story, as a whole, gives the impression of being rather a stock-piece; the detail of it is remarkably like that of the appearance of the 'Angel of Yahweh' to Gideon (Jud. 6: 11–24), and its purpose is obviously to enhance the supernatural element in the Samson figure. Since Samson displays no religious qualities whatso-ever, we may assume that the reference to the Nazir-ite vow is partly to explain his ecstatic fits (cf. Amos 2: 11) and partly to prepare for the hair-motif in the Delilah narrative. Probably the nativity narra-tive was part of the process whereby a series of stories

[18] Cf. Num. 6: 2–3. The word means 'one separated' or 'one consecrated'.

originally pagan was appropriated and made part of
the Hebrew tradition.

This leaves us with three stories about women. In
the first Samson enters into a liaison with a woman of
Timnah, of the kind known as a 'mota-marriage'—
that is, the woman remains in her father's home, and
the husband visits her from time to time, bringing a
present when he does so. But at the wedding feast
Samson is cheated by his new relatives in the matter
of a riddle, and he honours the debt thus unjustly
forced upon him by raiding a Philistine town and
collecting from thence the required amount of booty.
The first round may thus fairly be said to have gone
to Samson. The next move of the Philistines is to give
his newly-acquired wife to another man, and Samson
replies by catching three hundred foxes, tying them
in pairs, tail to tail, with a lighted torch stuck in the
knot, and then releasing them among the standing
corn of the Philistines in order to set their grain on
fire. This is sheer nonsense. Catching three hundred
foxes is itself a well-nigh impossible task, and the cruel
business of the tied tails and torches would, if it were
not too impractical to be real, be an act of sickening
cruelty. In any case, why not just fire the corn?
Obviously, the notion of three hundred demented foxes
careering with lighted torches through standing grain
is meant to appeal as being very funny. We whose not-
so-remote ancestors enjoyed bear-baiting and cock-
fighting, and whose contemporaries still indulge themselves in bull-fighting, can hardly afford to be too
superior in the matter, but at least we may be permitted to remark that, like Queen Victoria, we are
not amused. Certainly we cannot pretend to admire
the exploit. When the Philistines revenged themselves

75

on Samson by putting his quondam wife and her father to death—no one in the story appears to give *her* feelings a single thought!—Samson attacked them with great slaughter and then withdrew with all the honours to rest up in a cave.

If we are asked to accept this tale as literal truth, and the actions recorded in it as worthy of a man inspired by Yahweh, our credulity is strained beyond limit and our sense of what is moral refuses to permit us to applaud. There is not the slightest hint in the whole story of Samson having any spiritual superiority over his enemies, but only that he is physically superior. This is also the only conclusion to be drawn from the two pendants to the story (15: 9–20). In the first, Samson allows himself to be delivered bound to the Philistines by some Judeans, but then he breaks the rope as if it were flax and proceeds to slaughter a thousand of the enemy with the jaw-bone of an ass as a club. This is a Paul Bunyan story, if ever there was one, and is morally and spiritually on much the same level as that North American folk-tale. It evidently arose out of a place name, Assjaw, just as in the other pendant, the story of the spring is also an aetiology of a place name ('Caller's-well'). In due time, we may expect a Canadian aetiology of Moosejaw to be incorporated in the Paul Bunyan saga, and then we shall have a North American parallel indeed!

In the second tale, the woman in question is frankly a harlot, and his enemies hearing that he is visiting her surround the house to catch him as he leaves. But with a fine disregard for logic he escapes by walking off with the town gates and depositing them at Hebron some thirty miles away. This time we are in the premoral atmosphere of the Hercules legends, if not of the Irish giants who amiably threw rocks at one another so large that the hole left behind filled up with water and became a great lough. Put among those parallels, the story is clearly seen to be a naïve folk-tale of a prodigious feat of strength at which we can smile briefly and pass on. But if it were claimed to be anything more, then the moral character of this religious devotee who visits the harlot of Gaza would have seriously to be brought to question, and the logic of a situation whereby a man escapes from a surrounded house by walking off with the town gates on his shoulders would also have to be probed. Recognition of the story's folk-tale character allows us to be excused from these unrewarding enquiries.

And so we come to Delilah. It is said that there are only seven plots in all drama, and this is surely one of them—the heroic, trusting male who places his life confidingly in the hands of a paramour who cruelly betrays him. The childlike stature of the story is shown in the naïve artistry which carefully underlines the pattern in the repeated attempts of Delilah to entrap her lover, and in her repeated failures, until at last, by sheer female persistence, she wears him down and worms the fatal secret out of him. It is also shown in the impractical notion that three thousand (sic!) people on a roof supported by two central pillars could still be spectators of what was going on inside the house. More seriously, the completely non-religious nature of the tale is revealed when one reflects for a moment on the character of the god who either will not or cannot help his devotee if the Nazirite vow is broken by the cutting of his hair, even though he himself has not willed it. When we look for parallels to the Samson figure, we are hard put to it to find any in scripture,

77

but in the myths and legends of the world from which the Hebrews emerged, there is one character which is by no means unlike him. In the Gilgamish Epic[19] from Babylon, the hero is a tyrant-king whose subjects pray to the gods for a deliverer and they send them the wild, untamed strong man of the wastelands, Enkidu. He is, however, seduced by a harlot and, thus tamed, becomes the boon companion of Gilgamish and together they carry off many a boisterous feat of strength, until finally Enkidu is destroyed by another woman, the great goddess Ishtar. Samson is a strong man after the Enkidu pattern, and equally amoral.

There is, however, one notable element in the Samson stories which must not be overlooked. His feats of strength are credited to divine possession.[20] At this early period, the 'spirit of Yahweh' is thought of as a demonic power which takes possession of a man and gives him the ability to do the extraordinary. With some men it came as a power of leaderships as to Gideon; to others as the gift of 'second sight', as to Samuel; to others as an insight into God's will, as to Micaiah ben Imlah.[21] To Samson it came as the gift of immense physical strength. The religious poverty of the Samson stories is shown in that apparently he has no other finer qualities. He is completely individualistic and has no gifts of leadership, nor does he give any indication of spiritual or moral insight. The stories reveal in fact that the primitive notion of the Spirit of God taking possession of a man and enduing him with supernatural gifts was to undergo a long development before Paul could take pen and write 'the fruit of the

[19] Cf. *ANET*, p. 72.
[20] Jud. 13: 25; 14: 19; 15: 14.
[21] Jud. 6: 34–35; 1 Sam. 9: 19–20; 1 Kings 22: 17.

Spirit is love, joy, peace, patience, kindness, goodness, faithfulness, gentleness, self-control' (Gal. 5: 22–23).

There can be little doubt that the Samson stories survived because they were popular and satisfied a need. When the Philistines were in the ascendant and Israel could not retaliate in any effective way, these stories provided an emotional compensation to the prevailing sense of inferiority, just as the Robin Hood stories served the same purpose for Saxon England. After the Philistine menace had been averted, they remained popular as general encouragement to nationalist sentiment and because they illustrated vividly the cruder notions of the mysterious element in religion. When national sentiment and religious superstition are allied in a single theme, they form together a potent combination, and we do not have to seek any further for the reason for the survival of the Samson tales. The deuteronomists probably included them in their version of the Book of Judges because by the time they edited the older traditions, Samson was already robed in the sanctity of religious tradition.

It has been left to the honest enquiry of our own times to remove that wrapping, and to look at the Samson figure with candid sincerity. The little saga obviously lacks any sense of the theological purpose, such as is characteristic of myths like that of the First Man, or of the Flood; its psychological insight is superficial in comparison, for example, with that of the Jacob saga; and its religious content falls far below that of the cycle of stories concerning Elisha, though in many ways, these are the nearest parallel; if we are to be honest we have to say that the Samson story is frankly at the Arabian Nights level of entertainment. It is not surprising therefore that Saint-

79

Saens based an opera upon it (for in opera the story is notoriously unimportant) and that film producers have made (with skilful reshaping of the plot) a number of very successful 'biblicals' out of it.[22] The story does very well as a clothes-horse to hang melodies on, or as the scenario of a Hollywood 'spectacular', but if we are asked to take it seriously, the adult mind simply refuses to do so.

And yet until comparatively recently, mature and not uncritical minds did take the story seriously, and Samson was highly regarded as a man truly inspired by God. How are we to explain this? The answer I believe is extremely important. It is that so great is the power of religion that it can, unless we are very careful, make black look like white, the naïve appear profound, and the trivial appear to be of eternal worth. How else can we explain that Rahab the harlot, who played the traitress to her countrymen and delivered them over to utter destruction, simply in order to save her own skin, has been widely honoured in biblical and Christian tradition? If Jael had been playing for the other side, she would have been a despicable cheat, but because she was on 'our' side, she is a heroine. Again, how else can we explain that the Balaam story, talking ass and all, has been solemnly accepted for millennia as proof of Israel's election and providential history? Or how can we in any other way explain in learned commentaries of quite recent date the discussion of why Gideon was instructed only to choose those who lapped their water like a dog? The fact is that the power of religion to inhibit the critical facul-

[22] The latest production made Delilah the younger sister of the woman of Timnah, and so gave her a revenge motive for her treachery, a simple but extremely effective device.

ties and thus to suspend disbelief is so great that those of us who have grown up in its atmosphere have real difficulty in grasping its immensity. Religion can not only evoke faith but it can also induce credulity—and where does the one end and the other begin?

If therefore we ask with a slight twist of the old proverb 'is Samson also among the prophets?' meaning thereby what is this narrative doing in the canon of scripture alongside the high mythology of the First Man and the Flood, or the poetic profundities of Second Isaiah and the Psalter, or the stark narrative of the Crucifixion, my own answer would be twofold. First, it is there as background material, to show out of what origins Hebrew religion arose and to enable us to become aware of the towering heights to which other parts of scripture do rise up. The true height of Jerusalem is not readily understood while you stand in the Judean hill-country; but when you drop down to Jericho and look back, the realization of Jerusalem's elevation becomes very clear. It is indeed 'a city set on an hill'. Secondly, the Samson story is typical of much in scripture which is there to give us the opportunity to distinguish between credulity and faith, and then to force upon us the necessity of that distinction. It is faith which enters into the myth of the Magi, but it is credulity which accepts as literal history three kings guided by a moving star. To distinguish between the two is by no means always easy, but stories like those of Samson and Esther, at either end of Israel's history, are such as to force the problem upon us with crude bluntness. And once having recognized it, and as it were cut our teeth on these plain instances, we are then ready to move forward and consider the Elijah-Elisha narratives, and so, by way of the Red Sea and

81

the miracles of the New Testament, arrive at the heart of the problem, the Resurrection of Jesus Christ. It is a long journey from the night with the harlot of Gaza to the morning in the garden with an empty tomb, but it is one which we must make, for it is the road of our modern pilgrimage.

SAMUEL

And the people of Israel said to Samuel: 'Do not cease to cry to Yahweh our God for us, that he may save us from the hand of the Philistines.' So Samuel took a sucking lamb and offered it as a whole burnt offering to Yahweh; and Samuel cried to Yahweh for Israel, and Yahweh answered him.

Among the sayings of Jeremiah, there is a grim declaration that God has come to the end of His patience with Israel. He reports God as saying: 'Send them out of my sight and let them go! And when they ask you, "Where shall we go?" you shall say to them, "Thus says Yahweh———" ' and then follows the biblical equivalent of 'Go to hell'. Our present interest in this saying is that according to Jeremiah, God declares He is so determined on this course that He will not be diverted from it even though Moses and Samuel interceded for the condemned nation. Again in Psalm 99, Samuel alone is chosen to rank with Moses and Aaron as the great mediators between man and God.[23] Samuel is clearly then one of the outstandingly significant figures of the Old Testament.

Nevertheless, Samuel has been the subject of a good deal of scholarly discussion. This is because at least two sets of narratives are discernible in the first half of 1 Samuel and the estimate of the central figure is markedly different in the two strands of tradition. In the one,[24] we have the infancy narrative, the Ebenezer victory, the warning against appointing a king, the people's persistence, the choice of Saul by lot, Saul's installation at Gilgal, a solemn exhortation to him and the people at the beginning of the new institution, Saul's failure and rejection, and the divinely inspired

[23] 'Moses and Aaron were among his priests, Samuel also was among those who called on his name.' (Ps. 99: 6.)
[24] 1 Sam. 1–3; 7: 3–14; 8: 1–22; 10: 17–27; 11: 14—12:25; 13: 7b–15a; 15: 1—16: 13.

choice of David as his successor. In these passages Samuel is a regal figure, leading the people in matters military, civil, and religious, interceding for them before God and in His name making and unmaking kings. He is indeed worthy to rank with Moses. In the second group of passages[25] the rise of Saul's kingdom is seen as due to Philistine pressure, the adventitious incident of the Ammonite attack on Jabesh-Gilead, and the remarkable qualities of Jonathan. Samuel makes only a fleeting appearance as a local seer, of whom Saul had not previously even heard. Further we note that while it is said that he 'judged Israel' (1 Sam. 7: 15–17), his circuit is in fact a small group of Benjaminite settlements, within five or seven miles of each other. Thus the second group of narratives suggests a variant tradition in which Samuel was a very much smaller figure than in the first group.

That the Samuel of the first tradition is an idealized rather than an historical figure is further emphasized by the discrepancies between his reported activities and the subsequent historical actualities. For example, having called thunder from the sky, Samuel is said so to have inspired Israel with the virtue of success, that the Philistines were driven out of Israelite territory with such effectiveness that they did not re-enter it. Yet Saul's most persistent enemy, and the oppressor of Israel, and the foe to whom he and Jonathan finally fell was the Philistine invader. Again, although Samuel is credited with having been divinely guided to choose both Saul and David, in the subsequent narratives both come to prominence by deeds of courage which catch the nation's imagination. When we also note that the exhortations which Samuel delivers are clearly

[25] 1 Sam. 7: 15–16; 9: 1–10; 11: 1–11; 13: 1–7a; 13: 15b—14: 52.

deuteronomic in tone and style, we realize that we shall not be far wrong if we see in Samuel a cultic figure of no great national importance but of sufficient local significance to be capable of idealization by the deuteronomic historians. It is more than doubtful if we can get back to the historical person: he has been wholly subsumed—apart from his brief appearance in the second tradition—in the deuteronomic idealization.

Thus in considering Samuel our questions have to be these: what were the motives of those who built up this dominating, regal figure? What kind of a person did they set out to create? Here I think we need to bear in mind two points: first, the character of such idealizations and secondly the character of the men who gave this one its final form.

When we discussed Joshua, we saw that he is in fact a messianic figure, but that unlike other messianic speculations he is projected not into the future but into the past. Men idealized the past, long before they idealized the future, and in fact have continued to do so until the present. The Golden Age in the past is historically much older than the Kingdom of God in the future. Thus the idealization of Joshua is as much an inspired vision of 'Messiah' as for example the famous portrait in Isaiah 11. Similarly the account of Samuel in the first tradition is a projection into the past of an inspired idealization of one who fulfils a particular vocation in the divine economy of the people of God.

As for the authors of the Samuel-figure, we must observe that they are more correctly described as 'traditionists'; that is, they were men who had received their material as tradition, and felt themselves to a large extent bound by it. Samuel had undoubtedly grown considerably before he came into their hands. Some personalities become 'legendary' even in their own lifetime, and many truly historical persons enlarge by virtue of their own vitality and of their appositeness to the needs of following generations. Thus the 'authors' of the Samuel-saga were probably only making more pronounced a process of idealization which had been going on for some long time. The affinity of the sermonic exhortations of Samuel to those of Joshua and to the speeches of Moses in Deuteronomy mark these particular 'traditionists' as belonging to the school of historians who were responsible for the great saga Deuteronomy–Joshua–Judges–Samuel–Kings. They were probably active in the reigns of Hezekiah, Manasseh, and Josiah, and well into the post-exilic period. Deuteronomy is the book that sets out their theory concerning the character and institutions of Israel as the Covenant People and the four 'histories' are in the nature of practical illustrations of that theory. In effect they were saying 'These are the laws which Yahweh has laid down to condition the life of the holy nation and this is how obedience and disobedience to those laws works out in actual practice'. Therefore we are led to conclude that the clue to the significance of the Samuel-figure is to be found in the Book of Deuteronomy.

Now, Deuteronomy is a re-drawing of Israel's national and religious institutions in the light of the insights of the eighth-century prophets. Thus we often think of Deuteronomy as standing over against Leviticus, the great priestly document. In many ways this is true, but in many (perhaps more profound) ways it is quite false. They were both, one in the seventh century

88

and the other in the fifth, attempts to re-organize the life of Israel. Because in the seventh century, Israel was still a political state, a kingdom formulating its own laws, and controlling its own destinies, Deuteronomy has a wider range of interests than has Leviticus. The Priestly Corpus as a whole reflects the fact that in the post-exilic period, Israel had, in the well-known phrase, 'ceased to be a nation and had become a church'. Thus Leviticus strikes us as a more ecclesiastical, sacerdotal document than does Deuteronomy; but this must not obscure the fact that the main character of Deuteronomy is also cultic and sacerdotal. It ordains the centralization of the cult at Jerusalem and prescribes the character of Passover; it is solicitous for the welfare of the priesthood, which it is careful always to equate with the Levitical guild; it provides a ritual for the First-Fruits Thanksgiving, and details the laws of clean and unclean foods. It inculcates an abhorrence of all worship other than that given to Yahweh. Apart from these distinctive emphases, the book as a whole re-issues the Law of Yahweh, which is itself the content of *torah* or priestly instruction. From beginning to end, Deuteronomy is a priestly document, and Samuel is the deuteronomic idealization of the priest. We are told that he wore the ephod from his earliest years. He is also described as a prophet, which reminds us that the distinction between the two rôles was not held to be exclusive; Ezekiel also was both priest and prophet. But Samuel's main rôle was that of the priest.

We may be inclined to ask why, if this is so, the figure of the High Priest is not more prominent in Deuteronomy itself. The answer is that in monarchical times the office of High Priest had not evolved to anything like its post-exilic stature, and the chief priest at Jerusalem was probably still simply called 'the priest'.[26] While the King reigned there was no great scope for a 'high' Priest, but the office of 'the priest' was nevertheless highly regarded by many, and it is a sign of the times that they chose to depict their ideal for this office in a setting which did not contain an established monarchy. In the post-exilic period there were many who preferred living under the rule of the High Priest to living under the rule of a King, and for such people messianism had little attraction.

What then, are the significant features in this priestly portrait of Samuel? First, his passionate loyalty to Yahweh. In the land of conflicting cults, the deuteronomists were quite clear that there could not be any compromise at this point. We may regret such passages as Deut. 7: 1–7 and 1 Sam. 15 (the story of Samuel hewing Agag in pieces before Yahweh), but it is legitimate to point out that this is largely paper-ferocity. There were no physical Canaanites in the seventh century, since they had all long since become Hebrews and had been absorbed into Israel; but there were plenty of Canaanite ideas and tendencies. The deuteronomists were not inciting to physical atrocities on present elements in the population but were reacting violently against pernicious religious influences. The positive aspect of their apparent barbarity is a fierce loyalty to Yahweh, as summed up in the *Shema'*: 'Hear, O Israel, Yahweh our God is one Yahweh, and you shall love Yahweh your God with all your heart and with all your soul and with all your might.' No lukewarm predilection but a fervent love is what they seek to arouse.

[26] Deut. 10: 6; 26: 3; 2 Kings 11: 9.

It is this same characteristic which is expressed in the most contrived of all the Samuel stories, the Ebenezer incident. The chapter (1 Sam. 7: 3–14) relates how Samuel summoned the whole nation to repentance at Mizpah, but this gathering occasioned a Philistine attack. Samuel sacrificed and called on Yahweh for help, and the deity threw the enemy into panic so that they became an easy prey for the Israelites. As a monument to the occasion, Samuel set up a stone called 'The Stone of Help'. We may suspect that the stone was an ancient one and had acquired in pre-Hebrew times the name Eben-ezer (Stone of Help) because of help given to pilgrims to that spot. We may compare the modern pilgrimages to Lourdes. Our present story is an aetiological legend Hebraizing the Stone and its associations, just as the Christmas tree and Easter egg have long been Christianized in our own culture. But the theological intent is to emphasize the priestly function of Samuel, summoning the people to repentance because of idolatry, winning them to whole-hearted adherence to Yahweh, and dispensing 'salvation' in return.

Another marked aspect of the Samuel-figure is his activity as the oracle of God's will. By him is revealed the doom of the house of Eli, the rise and fall of Saul and the divine choice of the House of David. We normally associate the declaration of God's will with the prophets, but it was also a recognized function of the priesthood. The difference between prophet and priest lay rather in the means whereby God made His purposes known to them—to the prophet through ecstasy and the experience of possession, to the priest through the sacred lot and through dreams, probably induced by 'incubation', or sleeping in the holy precincts so that the dream might be more readily given. We recall the first occasion when the Word of Yahweh came to the boy Samuel. Certainly, the priest like the prophet was a man of God and as such could be appealed to in order to ascertain the divine will.

The best-known function of the priest is to offer sacrifice and we find Samuel serving the cultus both with peace-offerings and with burnt-offerings. These are the two forms of sacrifice which reflected two interpretations of the ancient ritual—in the first instance, that it was primarily a meal, which God and worshippers shared together as a sign of their community; and in the second, that it was the giving of a gift whereby God was propitiated and brought to look favourably on the sinner. But while it is taken for granted that Samuel as priest performs these sacrifices, the emphasis is significantly laid not here but on the moral demands of Yahweh. Samuel says to Saul:

> Has Yahweh as great delight in burnt offerings
>   and sacrifices
>   as in obeying the voice of Yahweh?
> Behold, to obey is better than sacrifice,
>   and to hearken than the fat of rams.
>
> (1 Sam. 15: 22)

The Cultic Revival which produced Leviticus had not yet taken place.

More characteristically, Samuel is the great intercessor. His ministry of prayer arises out of his pastoral concern for the people, and he is often to be found in prayer on their behalf. He pleads for Israel in her repentance and her danger at Mizpah; he brings their request for a king before Yahweh, and it is he who brings their subsequent penitence and fear before the offended deity. It is his continued intercession for them which averts the divine wrath (1 Sam. 12: 19–23), and as we have already seen, it is the rôle of intercessor which is stressed both in Jeremiah and in Psalm 99. As priest Samuel stands before God on behalf of the people, and as priest he stands before the people on behalf of God (1 Sam. 12: 7).

This then is the answer to our primary question: 'The deuteronomic historians were seeking to elaborate and idealize the rôle of the priest.' For some readers of the Bible, this recognition is a disappointing one. They respect, indeed glory in the revelation given to Israel through her prophets, but are suspicious of, if not strongly antipathetic to, her great priestly tradition. Perhaps, however, to see Samuel as the idealization of the priest will be a corrective to such thinking. The priestly tradition is a very large part of the Old Testament revelation and to be unreceptive of its contribution is to be deaf to much of the fullness of the Word of God. We have always understood that Jesus is to be interpreted in the light of His threefold office, Prophet, Priest and King. The rôle of prophet is richly understood because of the ministries of Isaiah, Jeremiah and the rest; the meaning of kingship is set forth for us in the great messianic tradition; but what content shall we put into the office of priest? When we see Samuel set forth as the pastor of his people, the declarer of God's will, the one who calls to devoted loyalty, and the intercessor on behalf of the nation, we can begin to understand what we mean when we talk of Christ our great High Priest. Nor may we forget that as priest Samuel offered the sacrifices of the people. These were the God-ordained means of expiation and reconciliation. By these, sin was dealt with, and fellowship with God renewed. Thus Samuel helps us to understand the meaning of that other sacrifice, offered by a Priest not of the House of Eli, nor of the House of Zadok, but as the writer to the Hebrews tells us, of that other, older line, the order of Melchizedek, priest of God Most High.

There is, however, another christological significance in Samuel. Of all the Bible stories few surpass in universal appeal the account of Samuel's early days. Hannah prayed so earnestly for a son that she was deemed to be drunken, but God heard her prayer and she called her child 'Samuel'. Like all Old Testament names, it had a meaning: 'The Name of God'. God's 'Name' in the Old Testament is His reputation, His character as it is known by what He has done. It is the summary of what He is; it is God in so far as He has revealed Himself. Thus Samuel is a living testimony to a profound truth: that God has a Name—He is not vague, mysterious and unknown, but is known and reverenced because He is always revealing Himself to men. And the truth to which the boy bears witness becomes a fact of his own experience. He grew up in the shrine at Shiloh, familiar with holy things, but having no personal knowledge of God. 'Samuel did not yet know Yahweh.' Then in the silence of the night, God called: 'Samuel, Samuel!' And when he realized who it was who called, he said: 'Speak, for thy servant is listening!'

From that time on, Samuel had not only heard of God, but knew Him for himself. God spoke to him, and he knew that it was God who had spoken. Once again the God of Israel had proved Himself I AM, the Living God. When Samuel arose, men knew that there was again a source of revelation in Israel. We may recall that the central significance of Jesus lies in that same truth expressing itself in another and yet more wonderful manner—that through a human personality the Almighty God reveals Himself to men. Samuel, 'Name of God', who was a living testimony to the self-revealing of God, prepares us for Jesus, who was Himself the Word of God become flesh.

Here, then, is Samuel as ancient tradition and modern scholarship present him to us. When a congregation today seeks for a minister whom they may call to have the cure of their souls, they enquire whether he is a listenable preacher, a conscientious visitor, a friendly man about the parish; and in so doing they are expressing the continual desire of the people of God for good and holy pastors. Samuel is the expression of that same desire, raised into the formulation of an ideal. As we see him caring for his people, teaching, rebuking, exhorting, offering their sacrifices, presenting their prayers, and interceding for them at the throne of grace, we recognize in him the Good Pastor and think of him who is the Good Shepherd.

SAUL

Thy glory, O Israel is slain upon thy high places!
  How are the mighty fallen!
Tell it not in Gath,
  publish it not in the streets of Ashkelon;
lest the daughters of the Philistines rejoice,
  lest the daughters of the uncircumcised exult.

How are the mighty fallen
  in the midst of the battle!

The account of the reign of King Saul marks a decisive change in the character of Old Testament narrative. Up to this point we have traditions which existed in oral form in the mind of Israel for generations. We have learnt recently a new respect for the historical element contained in such traditions, and *A History of Israel* by John Bright reflects this in sharp contrast to *The History of Israel* by Martin Noth, or even Oesterley and Robinson's older work of a generation ago.

Nevertheless, oral tradition conveys legends; it takes writing to convey history. Legends may contain a very great deal of history, and a reasonably sound account of historical events can often be built up from them, but their purpose is in general aetiological and their narratives are of isolated incidents, each forming its own literary unit, which may indeed be brought together to provide a portrait but never a biography, or may be strung together to indicate an outline but never a full history.

But somewhere round about the time of David and Solomon, the world's first historian was born—some five hundred years before Herodotus 'the Father of History' as R. H. Pfeiffer rightly points out. Internal evidence has even suggested his name: Ahimaaz the son of Zadok, the priest. Whether it was he or another, and whether it was he who was also the author of the Yahwistic source of the Pentateuch, are matters of interesting speculation, but there is no doubt that in the older source of the Book of Samuel we have a real attempt to write history. As to what constitutes the inner character of history, historians and their philosophers differ, but we may perhaps allow ourselves as a working definition 'the recounting of past events in such a connected way that their factual character is respected and their significance for the narrator is suggested'. In the light of such a definition, it is clear that the boundaries between legend and history will always remain fluid, and the historian as a *genus* will always range from Clarendon to Rancke, from the inconsiderately biased to the impersonally detached; but the historian who deserves the name at all will always seek the connexion between events, and will always respect their actuality. Such a writer was the author of the older account of Saul's reign and of the admiring but frank narrative of the reign of David and the accession of Solomon.

The older narrative as it is now commonly disentangled from the later source runs as follows.[27] An introductory legend concerning Saul's youth sought to link him from the first with Samuel, but probably he rose to fame when already a mature man because of his exploit at Jabesh-Gilead. The times were particularly bad for the Hebrews, since the old twelve-tribe amphictyony ('federation') had broken down completely under Philistine pressure. The central shrine at Shiloh had been destroyed, and the amphictyonic symbol, the Ark of Yahweh, had been ignominiously captured in battle. Israel was wholly at the mercy of her Philistine overlords. Various other peoples were

[27] I Sam. 9: 1—10: 16; 11: 1–13; 13: 1–7, 15b—14: 52; 16: 14–23; 18: 3–10, 17–29; 19: 11–17; 21: 1–9; 22: 6–23; 23: 1–14; 25: 2–44; 26: 1—27: 12; 28: 3–25; 31: 1–13.

taking advantage of her helplessness to press their own attacks upon her, and among them was Nahash the Ammonite, who sought to impose a particularly brutal and humiliating surrender on the Hebrew town of Jabesh, across Jordan in Gilead. When the news reached Saul he was taken with an ecstatic frenzy, collected a crowd of helpers, rushed off to Jabesh, and thoroughly routed the enemy. Hungry for a leader against the Philistines, the people brought him to Gilgal, another old amphictyonic shrine, and made him king.

His main task was to break the Philistine hold on the nation, and at first he was splendidly successful. Largely owing to his son Jonathan's courageous exploit, he gained at Michmash a notable victory, which restored control of the central highlands to Israel. He also campaigned against Amalek, and we hear of wars with Edom, Moab and Zobah. Unfortunately, Saul's volatile emotional states now took a despondent turn and he became a prey to a brooding melancholia; it was in order to relieve this by his musical skill that David was first brought into Saul's following. But the courage and success of David soon brought him a popularity which Saul felt threatened his own. Even his son Jonathan was attracted by the magnetic charm of the young soldier-musician, and Saul, now seriously alarmed, tried to kill him. When this failed, the king hit upon the scheme of offering David his daughter Merab as wife and through her a tentative right to be considered his heir, but only in exchange for a dowry in the collection of which David stood a very good chance of losing his life in battle. When the young hero survived this danger also, Saul was forced to honour his agreement, at least to the extent of giving David a younger daughter. But on the very wedding-night he again sought to kill his new son-in-law, and only the astuteness of the bride saved David's life. David fled to Nob, and the priests there who in all innocence gave him food and arms paid dearly for their mistake when Saul's men butchered them for helping him—only Abiathar escaped. David managed to protect Keilah from a Philistine raid, but grateful as the inhabitants were, they feared Saul's anger more, and knowing that he was not safe among them, David retreated into the foothill country. After the Nabal interlude, we have the exciting tale of how David and one of his men actually penetrated Saul's sentries and stole his spear and waterpot. From a safe distance David then awoke the camp and pointed out that he could easily have killed Saul, but had refrained. Saul, momentarily touched, gave up his pursuit, but David knew the mood would not last and sought more permanent security as a mercenary in the pay of the Philistines.

Saul's real business was with the Philistine threat to Israel's existence. His insane hatred of David had driven his strongest ally into the arms of the enemy and now he must face that enemy alone. He had lost his own sense of the blessing of Yahweh, and his attack on the priesthood had alienated the religious leaders to whom he might have turned for help. In desperation he resorted to a witch, and whether by her treacherous cunning or his own fevered imagination he heard his old mentor Samuel prophesy utter disaster in the battle to come. But Saul was never a coward, and although he knew the battle was lost before it was begun, he fought until all was hopeless and then committed suicide.

Even from this bald synopsis we can recognize that

we have here a remarkable piece of connected narrative, showing how one event led to the next and how the tragedy of Saul lay in the developing violence of his own nature. Without the waste of a word or the inclusion of an incident too many, the madness of Saul's determination to destroy David is made unmistakably clear. Yet to the end the author is careful to show that Saul retained something of his former stature. 'Ahimaaz' knew that, even in the ruin of his life, Saul remained a great man, and is honest historian enough to make sure that we also shall realize it. The Philistine exultation over Saul's death is a revealing estimate of what an enemy he had been to them, and what a strength to Israel. He had brought to birth in Israel a sense of unity she had never previously possessed. When he fell in battle, the glory of Israel was slain upon her high places.

'Ahimaaz' has in fact written a fine, a truly historical account of Saul and his fortunes. We are still left, indeed, with many uncertainties, and especially about the duration of Saul's kingship. The Hebrew of 1 Sam. 13: 1 can only be translated: 'Saul was one year old when he began to reign, and two years he reigned over Israel.' The first half of the verse is manifestly absurd, and the second half is grammatically suspect. The events described seem to require rather more than two years, but while some authorities think in terms of twenty years, and others guess at the decade before 1000 B.C., Martin Noth is content to accept the figure given. The account of Saul is history rather than tradition, but it is still in many respects very deficient.

In what sense then is there anything new in this narrative of the reign of Saul? The answer lies in the attitude we find ourselves taking towards him as distinct from that which we take towards the older figures. The latter have a symbolic significance, and their personality and the facts of their lives have been made frankly subservient to it. Abraham, Isaac, and Jacob symbolize the doctrine of Election, Joseph the doctrine of Providence, Moses the Covenant, Joshua the Messiah, Samuel the Priest—but Saul is simply Saul, a man to whom very strange things happened, a figure of great importance in the development of Israel's institutions, but nevertheless a figure whom you must accept as he is and whom you must not attempt to fit into any doctrinal mould. There are rich and varied lessons to be drawn from a thoughtful consideration of his story, but the lessons are in the mind of the beholder, not in the facts themselves, as they are in the Abrahamic saga, for example. Or, to put the same thing in another way, we theologize over Moses and Joshua, but we moralize over Saul.

This raises some very large problems of exegesis. We know, fairly well, the rules for theologizing. The great doctrines of Election, Providence, Covenant, Messiah, Priesthood, these have a history of debate, discussion and formulation. But moralizing—that is a different matter. One man's principle is another man's platitude. What is a basic conviction, the very ground of moral being, to one, is to another a mere generality. Again, we can never know what will suddenly catch our imagination and say to us 'Thou art the man'.

Yet moralize we must. That is what history is given us for. It is the past which supplies us with judgments for the present and perspectives for the future. We study history in order that we may have access to the accumulated experience of those who have gone before. It is from history that we draw the precepts whereby we discipline and inform our own decisions. But then again, we have to remember that we are not speaking of history as the activity of man alone. This history, which we embark upon with the story of Saul, is history in which God is as active as in the stories of the Patriarchs and Moses. We cannot draw a distinction between 'sacred history' and 'profane', but we can say that in this history God's purpose, His judgment, and His mercy have long since been discerned and made apparent to us. For it is clear that 'Ahimaaz' did not write his history of the rise of the kingship to have no meaning at all. He meant his story to have a very clear moral. Our problem is to discern it aright.

This brings us to a consideration of the later source in the Saul material.[28] Here we have the stories of how Saul was reluctantly chosen king by Samuel after recourse to the divine lot, and of how, although duly fortified with a rather morose sermon, he straightway proved himself unworthy by presuming to offer sacrifices rather than wait for Samuel. We are also told how he presumed to disobey the direction of the man of God in the matter of the dreaded 'ban' whereby everything so cursed must be utterly destroyed, and how David was chosen by Samuel under divine prompting to replace Saul. It is this later source which includes the memorable story of David and Goliath, and the unconsciously humorous one of how, when Saul's jealousy was aroused by David's popularity and he sought to kill him, first the royal messengers and then the king himself were made helpless by being caught up in the ecstatic frenzy of the prophets among

[28] 1 Sam. 10: 17–27; 12: 1–25; 13: 7b–15a; 15: 1–35; 17: 1–58; 19: 18–24; 24: 1–22.

whom David had taken refuge. The final story tells how Saul's life was spared by David in a cave near Engedi and how Saul was shamed into generosity and himself promised David the succession to the kingship. This appears to be the conclusion of the late source and gives us the clue to its character. Its purpose is to vilify Saul in order to justify David, and to emphasize that the divine favour which had been so signally withdrawn from Saul now rested in abundant measure upon his successor. But why should men who come some three long centuries after the time of both Saul and David want to give this added bias to the remarkably fair account of 'Ahimaaz'?

The answer is that they were doing what we have recognized that we must do also; they were moralizing on the story. They saw in the stories of the two men a powerful illustration of the way in which the judgment of God is at work in the lives of all men, great and small. David prospered in all his ways, and therefore, they said, he must have been a good man and obedient to the divine prompting. Saul was an unhappy, tragic figure, and therefore, they thought, he must have been disobedient. To bring this out they emphasized the rejection of Saul, and in particular they inserted the stories of his two outstanding 'crimes'—the usurpation of the priestly privilege of sacrificing, and the arrogant modification to his own liking of the divine command which he had received to put Amalek to the ban.

Here then is guidance to our question of how we ought to draw the moral from the story of Saul. The moral clearly is 'God rejects the arrogant'. But are we as Christians prepared to accept such guidance? Is historical truth to be adapted, we might even say perverted, to suit the needs of later moralizing in this way? At this point, the historical character of biblical revelation comes into play from another direction. These moralizers were children of their own times, in which the historical sense was as yet only just beginning to develop. We who look back on a long historical tradition must have a reverence for historical fact which we cannot expect of them. They saw that history should teach men how they ought to live. They recognized that we must learn the lessons of the past in order ourselves to live rightly in the future. To them it seemed justifiable to go back and blacken the greys and cleanse the somewhat murky white. In all honesty, we cannot copy them in this. But although we cannot adopt their methods, we can follow in the direction to which they point. We can realize that what they attempted, we must also attempt, and in the light of our clearer Christian insights do rather better.

What then shall our moral judgment be on Saul, King of Israel? First, it will be one of sympathy for a man, a great man, courageous and noble, who responded generously to the call to serve his people in their time of need. But we shall also try to see where this great man went wrong: not in pretensions to some priestly or prophetic rank which he did not possess, but rather in a much more common fault. He was jealous. It was indeed self-pride which brought about his fall. His declared aim was to deliver his people from the Philistine menace. When therefore his young lieutenant began to rival his own prowess, he ought, had he been thinking of the common good, to have rejoiced in the new accession of strength, in the new gifts of leadership and of valour. His failure is all the more striking because we are shown in Jonathan just that self-denying devotion whereby he was prepared to forgo his own prominence and if necessary to serve under David. Saul, on the other hand, could not bring himself to share his own position with the newcomer. His pride demanded that either he must save Israel, or it were better that Israel should go down in defeat on Mount Gilboa. But there is a stern judgment of God on such pride, and Saul brought that judgment down upon himself.

It is a damning sin when we put our position, our pride, our jealous anger before the service of the purposes of God. It is a destroying sin but not an uncommon one. We meet jealousy in modern politics, in business, in the life of the Church, and always it is destructive. That is why Saul is a significant figure. He reminds us that there is a judgment of God upon the proud.

DAVID

And David said longingly: 'O that someone would give me water to drink from the well of Bethlehem which is by the gate!' Then the three mighty men broke through the camp of the Philistines, and drew water out of the well of Bethlehem which was by the gate, and took and brought it to David. But he would not drink of it; he poured it out to Yahweh, and said: 'Far be it from me, O Yahweh, that I should do this. Shall I drink the blood of the men who went at the risk of their lives?'

There is a story that when Sir William Orpen was asked to paint the portrait of Cosmo Lang, then Archbishop of York, he said: 'But which Lang do you want me to paint? In that face I can see at least seven different men.' The completed portrait, comments his biographer, was that of the proud prelate, rather than one of those other Langs whom his friends knew and loved.

When I set out to lecture or write about David that story comes readily to mind. Which David am I to choose? For of all the personalities of the Old Testament none has so many different aspects to his character as David, nor indeed has suffered so many transformations at the hands of posterity. To use a truly biblical idiom, if Lang is sevenfold, then David is seventy-sevenfold.

There are, for example, two quite different accounts of how he came to prominence. The first tells how Samuel was directed by Yahweh to anoint David as Saul's successor, even though he was the youngest of eight—a folk-tale touch, whereby the ugly duckling becomes the most beautiful swan of all.[29] In the story as it continues, however, David is incongruously not the young and inexperienced shepherd-boy of the earlier verses, but is already renowned for his skill on the harp and, as a mature and seasoned warrior, he is invited to join Saul's entourage.[30] In the other older

[29] I Sam. 16: 1–13, possibly seventh century.
[30] 16: 14–23, possibly a later addition.

III

story he is again a simple unregarded shepherd-lad (but of remarkable deuteronomic orthodoxy) who rose to prominence by slaying the giant Philistine, Goliath of Gath.[31] As they now stand these stories cannot both be true. If David was Saul's beloved armour-bearer in 16: 21, Saul could not have been so ignorant as not even know his name in 17: 55; if on the other hand the events of 17: 1f. are held to precede those of 16: 14f., then Saul would not have needed to send for David (16: 19), for he had already attached him to his house (18: 2)! Moreover, Goliath was in fact slain by Elhanan son of Jaareoregim.[32] David has attracted the story to himself, and clearly the traditions have grown with the passing years. The probable truth is that David was a local bandit-chief who was successful enough to attract Saul's attention, and was thus attached to the newly-formed court where he quickly rose to prominence, but in so doing roused Saul's jealousy. The story of Samuel picking him out early and actually anointing him was designed to add divine predestination to his prestige, and also no doubt to attach the Yahweh-cult firmly to the coat-tails of this rising star. The Goliath story was borrowed from Elhanan and worked up to further the same two interests.

As tradition thus sought to use its creative powers to reshape David's youth, so too it sought to present his whole character and personality in accordance with

[31] 17: 1—18: 2, also containing later additions.
[32] 2 Sam. 21: 19. The Chronicler, recognizing the difficulty inserted 'Lahmi the brother of' before Goliath (1 Chron. 20: 5) and this in turn gave rise to the italicized insertion 'the brother of' in the AV of 2 Sam. 21: 19. RSV translates the true text. Another ingenious suggestion is that Elhanan is David's real name and that 'David' is only a name (or possibly a title?) which he assumed on coming to the throne. But how comes it that his real name has survived only here? And that he has also acquired a different father?

its own needs. The later, deuteronomic source in 1 and 2 Samuel is thus already to be found presenting David not as a man but as an institution, the Royal Messianic House. We see this, for example, in the narrative in which David is credited with desiring to build the Temple, that is a 'house' for God, but is told to leave this task to his son; for he will have a son to follow him on the throne (2 Sam. 7: 1–29). It is God who is going to build a house, David's 'house', as a continuing royal line forever. The whole passage obviously owes much to Psalm 89: 19–37. Together they explain how 'David' became a name for the continuing and enduring institution of royalty. When we read, for example: 'I will set up over them one shepherd, my servant David . . . and I Yahweh will be their God, and my servant David shall be prince among them. . . . (Ezek. 34: 23–24), we are not to think of David personally, *redivivus* as in the Nero or Barbarossa or Arthur legends, but of David as an institution, a corporate personality, the Royal House. It is interesting to notice that so powerful did this tradition become that Jesus was forced to protest against it: if, he said, the most important thing about the Messiah is his Davidic descent, then obviously David is greater than the one who depends on him for his significance. Yet everyone knows that Messiah is greater even than David—does not the royal author of the psalter himself address the Messiah in those psalms as 'my lord'? There must clearly be more to the Messiah than simply that he is David's son (Mark 12:35f.). The protest was as necessary as it was timely, but it is revealing testimony to the strength of the institutional aspect of David's reputation.

A parallel development was that of David as the great ecclesiastic. How came it that the Temple was not built in David's time but in Solomon's? By the time of the Chronicler (third century B.C.) the Temple was so much the centre of Jewish life that to think of it as not being related to David was quite impossible. We have already seen that a good deal earlier the suggestion was abroad that, of course, David wanted to build the Temple and only desisted on a direct divine command. The Chronicler goes much further. David is not allowed to build the house because he is a man of war, and Solomon a man of peace shall build it, but David will make preparation for it, supplying plans, building materials and workmen. Moreover, before he dies, he arranges carefully the Levitical order, and determines who shall serve in the Temple, and especially in the choir. Here then is another David, the Royal Founder and Benefactor, the wise Ecclesiastic, to whom all the liturgical and cultic life of the Temple owes its inspiration and origin.

We have already had a reference to yet another development of the David-figure. One of the Levitical choirs used a collection of psalms which was called 'David's Collection'. Others were the Asaphite and Korahite collections and just as not all the Asaphite repertoire was the work of Asaph, nor all the Korahite collection the work of Korah, so too the Davidic collection need not necessarily have been wholly of David's composing. Many psalms labelled Davidic are clearly not written by him. But his name became more and more associated with the Psalter as a whole until it was simply assumed that if no other name was attached then the psalm was David's. Jesus naturally adopts the convention and says 'David himself, inspired by the Holy Spirit, declared . . .', meaning simply 'in the inspired psalter, it says . . .'

This attribution of the psalter to David had two main results. First that David became the poet *par excellence* of the Hebrew people, but more importantly, that the experiences reflected in the psalms were naturally attributed to their 'author'. Since the majority of psalms are laments of the righteous men in distress, David was now viewed as the innocent, persecuted sufferer, hated by his enemies, betrayed by his friends, helpless before overwhelming disasters, but loyally and fervently trusting in God to deliver him. There is something peculiarly pathetic and appealing in the thought of royalty calumniated and ill-used (it was the greatest asset the Stuart pretenders possessed) and some of us can still remember bible-illustrations of a woe-begone David seated alone in a cave, dressed in royal robes and crown, with a harp in his hand and an appropriate verse from the psalms in his mouth. To link him with the suffering Servant of Isaiah 53 was a short step, but there is no evidence to show that it was ever taken before Christian times.[33] Under the influence of the Christian interpretation of that chapter, however, David and the Servant easily coalesced and the rôle of David as the Royal, Messianic Sufferer, the type of Jesus himself was fully complete.

How much in all this varied development reflects the real personality of the historic David? As we have often stressed in this series of Old Testament portraits, traditions inimical to the real character of a man do not easily attach themselves to him. In the case of David, the original personality was so rich and many-

---

[33] Some modern scholars have attempted to show that this identification was pre-christian, but not in my opinion successfully. That the figure of David as Royal Sufferer was pre-christian is shown by the Hebrew psalm-titles.

sided that all these later developments find ready justification in the historical figure. Moreover, we have excellent testimony to the historic person because of the famous 'Court-History',[34] a contemporary record of his reign which ranks among the world's masterpieces of literature. It tells the story of David vividly and intimately and while it certainly presents him as hero, it also reveals him as a very human personality. As Cromwell adjured Lely to paint him honestly, 'warts and all', so the Court Historian gives us a very frank and honest account of this tremendous personality. For let there be no doubt about it: David is one of the few truly dominating figures of all history. Only a man really great in his own person could have borne the weight which tradition laid upon him and still remain a recognizably human person.

It is not surprising that the belief in 'good luck' and 'bad luck' is so widespread for it gives a ready account of a phenomenon which is displayed persistently in human affairs at every level. Some men distil about them constantly the aroma of success just as surely as others carry about them the odour of failure. The answer may lie in the fortuitous combination of natural endowment, temperament, and opportunity, or it may be that divine providence calls on men to play different rôles in life, but certainly some seem consistently to succeed, to triumph over adversity and turn it to their constant advantage, and others with equal ability, virtue and industry seem doomed persistently to fail. The Hebrews were in no doubt that the determinative factor was the divine will. If a man was in good standing with God, if the divine blessing lay richly upon him, then in whatever he set out to do

[34] 2 Sam. 9–21; 1 Kings 1–2.

he would succeed. To prosper was to give evidence of
God's favour. To be outstandingly successful was to
have the aura of divine approval.

David, particularly in his younger days, had a
vitality which at all times gave him the virtue of success. We see it in that mysterious quality which made
him a natural leader of men. A brave and bonny
fighter, he had a touch of the romantic about him
which bound his soldiers to him personally. When he
longed for a drink from his home-well in enemy-held
Bethlehem and three of his men risked their lives to
get it, he rose to the occasion by pouring it out as a
drink-offering to Yahweh. A lesser man would have
drunk it with effusive thanks and a scattering of
largesse, but David lifts the whole incident on to the
plane of the sacred and eternal—and emerges a truly
heroic figure in the eyes of his followers. When Nabal
refused to play his part in David's 'protection-racket'
and the bandit-chief came down in wrath to make an
example of him, he was turned from his purpose by
a present and a woman's tear-filled eyes glistening in
the moonlight—but the husband obligingly died of
apoplexy on hearing of his narrow escape, and David
married the beautiful widow, inherited the farm, and
secured into the bargain a reputation for generosity
and forgiveness. Even when things are going badly for
him, and Saul is hunting him to death, David manages
to emerge with an enhanced reputation—did he not
twice have opportunity to slay Saul, and most nobly
forbear? Since he was not yet ready to take over Saul's
position, it was in any case very much to his advantage
to let Saul go on to make his own failure. David must
not seem in any way to contribute to it. So he gained
both material advantage and an increased reputation

by letting the king go unharmed. When the final battle between Saul and the Philistines is imminent and David is summoned to serve his overlord and join in the fight against Saul, and so put himself forever in the wrong with Israel, he was saved from having to make a choice between two equally disastrous alternatives by the other Philistine leaders. 'We don't trust him,' they said, 'he might change sides in the battle.' So while Saul went down in defeat, David was away gathering further renown in the affair of Ziklag. David had at all times the splendid virtue of success.

Thus it was that rather reluctantly the northern tribes had to acknowledge the inevitable and invite him to be king over them, too. The northern Hebrews had no great love for the Jews and in the Israelite Confederation the tribe of Judah had always been odd-man-out, but there was no viable alternative, and now that David had made the non-Jewish city of Jerusalem his capital they could accept him without loss of face. In him they recognized the prosperity which betokens divine blessing. Absalom, indeed, won their fickle hearts away for a brief while, but not for long, and while David lived he had no real rivals for the throne. It was he who established the nature, character, and style of kingship in Hebrew thought, he who enabled the idea of 'the Kingdom of God' to take root among them, he who established a royal house for four hundred years, and he who made possible the messianic idea.

And yet the uniformly successful man, the glittering child of fortune, while he may excite envy, seldom arouses love. David's success was tinged with enough of sorrow and calamity to keep him human, likeable, even at some moments pitiable. His infatuation for

Bathsheba, his inept efforts to cover up his crime, his desperate strategem to get rid of Uriah, these, strangely enough, in a character like David's do not repulse but rather endear. Uriah is testimony to that. He must have known all about his wife's adultery: he knew very well what the King was trying to get him to do; and while he could not bring himself to do that, he nevertheless consents to his own death, so strong is the King's hold over those immediately about him. And when Bathsheba's child was dying, all Jerusalem, privy to the whole affair, genuinely grieved with him; then when he rose and washed and put the whole matter from him, they all said: 'How right! He made a mistake, and he has paid for it, and now he can forget all about it. What a real man he is!' David understood well the morality of his people. But in his inability to control his family, and his daughter's shame, and his son's murder, and above all in that tragic cry: 'O my son Absalom, my son, my son Absalom! Would I had died instead of you! O Absalom, my son, my son!' in these things all Israel heard the voice of deep and bitter tragedy. There was that in David's life on which the legend of the Royal Sufferer could take firm hold.

Nor is the rôle of psalmist out of character. Two little laments, the one over Saul and Jonathan and the other over Abner, have survived as indisputably David's work and if these, why not other poems? The time is long since when it was dogma to assign all psalms to the post-exilic period. Indeed some are now thought to be borrowings from the Canaanites and possibly older than Israel herself. While it takes a bold man to say which psalms are of David's composing, or (what is more probable) what fragments of his work have been built into later poems, there is nothing out of character in making him 'the Father of Israel's Psalmody'. If it is not David speaking in some verses of Psalm 18 for instance, then someone else is very cleverly speaking in his tones:

> For who is God, but Yahweh?
>> And who is a rock, except our God?—
> the God who girded me with strength,
>> and made my way safe.
> He made my feet like hinds' feet,
>> and set me secure on the heights.
> He trains my hands for war,
>> so that my arms can bend a bow of bronze.
> Thou hast given me the shield of thy salvation,
>> and thy right hand supported me,
>> and thy help made me great.

Those verses express a genuine trust in Yahweh and a delight in him. A little earlier the psalmist asserts 'with the loyal Thou dost show Thyself loyal', and this is the most characteristic feature of David's whole career and personality. From the beginning he is devoted to Yahweh, and he believes all his success is due to Yahweh, and his triumph is equally Yahweh's triumph also. Only when David became King of all Israel, did Yahweh become indisputably the God of all Palestine. When David captured Jerusalem, he brought up the sacred Ark and established it in a tabernacle there and all Israel knew that from now on Yahweh was God of the whole land. In that act there lay pregnant the Temple and its cultus, the sanctity of Sion, and the strange fascination of Jerusalem as the Holy City, to Jew, to Christian, and to Moslem alike. Doubtless David would have been surprised could he have foreseen his future rôle as 'the Royal Saint', but he could not have disavowed it. Rather, he deserved it.

And what of David for us? Clearly here is no tidy and moral example of which we may say: 'Go thou and do likewise!' Few of us have the sheer ability to be a David, and still fewer have that rare gift of personality which enabled him to exploit so brilliantly both his own abilities and the situation in which he found himself. But as I review once again this truly royal character, so alive, so commanding, so successful, so honestly devoted to Yahweh, I am reminded of a conviction borne in upon me by so many biblical characters and incidents: that Life is something to be taken into our hands and made something of. It was never meant to be accepted passively, but rather to be the arena in which we aim at high ambitions, the stiff clay which we wrestle into the shape of our own dreams, the tough battle in which we give and receive telling blows, and stand to win or lose our all. And if a man will launch out into that understanding of life, with an intent to serve God and co-operate with Him, he may come to high attainment, or he may fall short of it, but the sense of divine blessing will be with him, and he will discover as David did, that 'with the loyal Thou dost show Thyself loyal'. Or, as Paul put it, 'if God be for us, who is against us?'.

SOLOMON

Judah and Israel were as many as the sand by the sea; they ate and drank and were happy. And Judah and Israel dwelt in safety, from Dan even to Beer-sheba, every man under his vine and under his fig tree, all the days of Solomon.

Not even Solomon, in all his glory, was arrayed like one of these!' With one deft phrase Jesus made all men aware of the beauty of the wayside flower. At the same time, he fixed the portrait of Solomon in the minds of men unforgettably as 'the Magnificent'. That is how all men will think of Solomon for ever.

In a way, it is the true portrait of him. There was, of course, much more to Solomon than the robes and jewels and furnishings of royalty, but more than most monarchs he made these things part of himself—the characteristic part of himself. Like Henry VIII, he was a king with a histrionic touch, who enjoyed playing the rôle of a king, and never for a moment relinquished the part. The result is that the trappings of pomp and circumstance have largely prevented us from recognizing the solid achievements of a very shrewd personality. On the other hand, they have also distracted attention from the fact that Solomon lost what David had so painstakingly achieved. The deuteronomic historians who compiled the Book of Kings were dazzled by Solomon and painted the most idyllic pictures of his reign,[35] but they also gave us the facts, and the facts speak for themselves.

Solomon was the child of Bathsheba. Possibly that is the most significant fact about him. Life in a royal harem in the ancient days was no idyll. The rivalries and jealousies of the women competing for the king's

[35] e.g. 1 Kings 4: 25.

favour were intense and ran deep, for so much was at stake. The lucky one would see her son succeed to the throne and she herself would become the First Lady in the land—for 'queen' meant little in a polygamous society, but Queen-Mother meant a very great deal. As for the others, they would not merely have lost out in the great competition, but might very well have lost life itself. The successful claimant to the throne often consolidated his position by murdering all his rival brothers. Life in a harem contained elements which when activated by external events set off a fearful destruction. We may recall how one Judean Queen-Mother, Athaliah, when she heard that her son had been slaughtered by Jehu, killed off the rest of the royal family and seized power herself for six years. But she only delayed her murder; she did not prevent it. When Bathsheba heard that one of Solomon's brothers had practically succeeded David, she told the King that this was a threat to her life and Solomon's. Undoubtedly, she was right. When Solomon was safely on the throne, he found means of getting rid of his brother and his chief supporters, even Joab, David's great lieutenant, and Abiathar his faithful priest.

So then, the fact that Solomon was Bathsheba's child was immensely important to him. It meant that he was the child of the most forceful personality in the harem and one of the most important in the royal entourage. As the ancient Rabbis remarked long since, a woman does not bath where she may be overlooked, unless it be of set purpose; and it was their opinion that Bathsheba deliberately sought to attract David's attention and to seduce him. Once in the palace, she set out to achieve her ambition and obtained David's promise that he would nominate her child as his successor.

When Adonijah grabbed prematurely at the crown, it was not Solomon but Bathsheba who organized the counter-plot and persuaded David to accept Solomon as co-regnant with him.

It was through his mother then that Solomon received the throne. Unfortunately it was not her only gift. She was a Jerusalemite. Her husband was a Hittite, an immigrant from the north; she may have been Hittite also, but more probably was Jebusite like the majority of Jerusalem's inhabitants. The city had not been in Hebrew hands long enough for the population to be anything else. Her religion was, then, originally not the worship of Yahweh, though she presumably adopted a nominal Yahwism after the conquest of Jerusalem. Other women in the harem were also from Jerusalem and one at least was an Arabian. Instead of the truly Hebrew upbringing of Adonijah, and the other sons born during David's Hebron days, Solomon received his early impressions in a cosmopolitan harem. It would not be surprising if he was not as wholeheartedly Yahwistic as David (1 Kings 11: 5).

There was one other grave disadvantage with which Bathsheba endowed her son. He was not a Hebrew. Physically, he was half-Hebrew through David, but mentally, possibly spiritually, he was never Hebrew. Had he been born earlier in David's life, nearer to the cave at Adullam or even during the Hebron period, he would have understood the men of Israel far better than he did. A gentile king could trade an area of land to another king in return for some advantage elsewhere, and no one would think much about it; but when Solomon ceded twenty Galilean villages to Hiram of Tyre to settle a debt, he deeply offended against the

127

Hebrew feeling for 'Israel', the sacred and chosen nation, the *qahal*, the 'congregation' of God. No man should be put out of the sacred fellowship simply because some king or other wanted to settle his debts. Again, if Solomon had understood the Hebrew mentality better, he would not have sold Hebrew slaves to Egypt in return for horses,[36] nor would he have put his subjects to the hated forced-labour (1 Kings 5: 13–16). True, the deuteronomic editors are careful to say that this was required only of Canaanites, not of Hebrews, but the Hebrews knew better, as they made quite clear when Rehoboam attempted to follow in his father's unpopular ways.[37] Solomon was, in fact, the son of his mother—colourful, gifted, resourceful, ambitious, ruthless. Had it not been for her, he would probably not have become king—or even survived his father's death; had it not been for her, he would probably not have been such a brilliant, successful king; but had it not been for her, he might not have made the fatal mistakes he did.

The achievements of Solomon were nevertheless remarkable. He established a close relationship with the reigning Pharaoh, who regarded him with favour and probably thought of him as a vassal. He occupied and rebuilt several of the old Egyptian fortresses, and the famous stables at Megiddo are an eloquent witness to the care and attention he bestowed on the garrisons he placed in them. He rebuilt the defence of Jerusalem, and especially the Millo or 'keep'; he also built a remarkable palace-complex, with its House of the Forest, its Hall of Pillars, its Hall of Judgement, its

---

[36] Deut. 17: 14–17 is probably a portrait of Solomon.
[37] 1 Kings 12: 12f, but especially v. 18. This contrasts with 9: 15–22.

royal apartments and harem, and the special harem for the daughter of the Egyptian Royal House, with whom Solomon had been honoured. Another part of the complex was the royal shrine, a temple dedicated to the national God, Yahweh. It is doubtful if Solomon knew what he had begun when he added that Chapel Royal to his palace.

Even more remarkable were his trading activities. His little kingdom lay astride the lines of communication of the ancient world. The routes, Arabia to Egypt, Egypt to Syria or Anatolia or Mesopotamia, Tyre to Damascus, or Tyre to the Red Sea and to the strange lands that lay beyond, Solomon dominated them all. He not only levied his taxes on the goods flowing through his dominions, but he also himself contributed greatly to the flow of merchandise. He found he could do a good trade in buying and selling horses and also in distributing in the north the greatly desired Egyptian chariots. He reckoned to pay one hundred and fifty talents for a horse and six hundred talents for a chariot, but we are not told his selling prices. Probably (despite 1 Kings 10: 28) he bought the horses in the north and sold them in Egypt, and the chariots he bought in Egypt and sold in the north, and made a handsome profit both ways.

Another venture was equally successful. 'King Solomon's Mines' were not the fabulous diamond deposits of fiction, but were, in fact, copper mines, especially in the Trans-jordan hills. At Aqaba on the Red Sea have been found the largest smelting furnaces of the period and though little is said in the Book of Kings about his mining interests, Solomon's activity in this matter must have been extremely important in his own day. It was the first sign of a backward people catching up with and benefiting from the best technology of the day. No doubt, King Solomon's Mines also produced the valuable iron which was still a fairly recent and extremely valuable newcomer to the economy and daily experience of the population of Palestine.

The best known of his trading adventures is, however, the partnership with Hiram of Tyre, whereby they financed and dispatched trading vessels down the Red Sea, to trade with the South Arabian ports and the mysterious, distant shore of East Africa. This was the location of that ancient land from whence Solomon obtained the variety of gold prized above all others— the gold of Ophir. With all this wealth pouring into his land, Solomon was able to build splendidly and play the part of a king magnificently.

And yet his successes were more superficial than real. Already in his own time, the cracks in the brilliant façade were beginning to show. A change of dynasty in Egypt gravely affected his political position. The new Pharaoh had dreams of reviving the ancient Egyptian empire in Palestine and therefore was bent on breaking up the Hebrew Kingdom. At first, he made no open attack, but he gave sanctuary and help to Solomon's enemies. When Jeroboam ben-Nebat, one of Solomon's protégés, was chosen by the prophet Ahijah to lead the revolt stirred up by the King's burdensome rule, Solomon tried to arrest him, but he escaped and found a ready welcome in Egypt, where he was given a pension and told to wait for the opportunity which would surely be his, sooner or later. During the later years of Solomon's reign, Jeroboam was thus a constant threat to the unity of the Hebrew Kingdom and on Solomon's death the threat materialized in the loss of the northern tribes. Probably it was the Egyptian army which forced Rehoboam to acquiesce in the setting up of the Northern Kingdom; otherwise he could have crushed the revolt fairly easily (1 Kings 14: 25).

There were at least two other indications that Solomon could not hold together the empire his father had left him. A claimant to the throne of Edom had escaped David's destruction of the Edomite Royal House, and he too was an honoured guest in Egypt, awaiting the propitious moment to return and force Edom's independence from Hebrew control. Whether he was successful in Solomon's time or whether he, too, had to wait until Solomon's death we do not know, but the threat of revolt was present all the time. Another local patriot made good his claim to independence quite early in Solomon's reign: Rezon ben Eliada set himself up as king in Damascus and revived the Syrian kingdom which David had overthrown.

But the most serious cause for anxiety was undoubtedly that Solomon never won the affection of the northern tribes but rather their resentment and hostility. He sought to erase the old tribal divisions by dividing the country into twelve administrative areas which ignored the old boundaries and loyalties, and appointed over them twelve officers who were in fact District Tax Collectors. It was as if Oliver Cromwell had sought to destroy the clan-structure of the Scots by extending his system of rule by major-generals into a re-drawn Scotland. With all their faults, the Stuarts would never have made such a mistake as that, because they knew their Scots; and David would similarly never have aroused hostility by such a measure, because he knew his Hebrews. But Solomon, the child of Bathsheba, did not. His ideas of kingship were merely oriental and despotic, and so he destroyed David's greatest achievement, the unity of the Hebrew tribes.

And yet Solomon gained the reputation of being very wise. This is brought out in the story of his prayer for wisdom at Gibeah at the time of his accession; and again in the legend of his shrewdness in the case of the two mothers claiming the same child, and yet again in the Arabian Nights incident of the visit of the Queen of Sheba. There was undoubtedly something in Solomon for these traditions to fasten on. He was shrewd in business matters, and seems to have got the better of the bargain with King Hiram of Tyre, for example (1 Kings 9: 10–14). He was astute in his administrative affairs and amassed considerable wealth. He also maintained sufficient military strength to suppress, as long as he was on the throne, all revolt from within or attacks from without. He had a fluency in the prized art of aptly quoting proverbs, and had some poetic gift: 'he also uttered three thousand proverbs; and his songs were a thousand and five'. He was apparently a man of many parts and has some claim to being the patron of natural scientists: 'he spoke of trees, from the cedar that is in Lebanon to the hyssop that grows out of the wall; he spoke also of beasts and of birds and of reptiles and of fish' (1 Kings 4: 33). It was on this aspect of tradition that his reputation in matters occult was based and in Arabic folk-lore he was destined to become the great magician.

Further, he built the Temple. Intended at first as a Chapel Royal attached to a palace-complex, a

St. George's, Windsor, as it were, it became the Westminster Abbey, and more, of the nation. It became the one place in the country where cultic worship could rightly be offered to Yahweh, the one locus where God was sacramentalized and made apprehensible for ordinary men. Here was the place where God was available. Men must have shrines, and sacred days, and sacramental media, and liturgical patterns, and Solomon provided for these needs when he built the Temple and established the order of its worship. He provided for them richly; he provided for them far better than he knew. But *was* he wise? The more you consider the many-sided complex traditions and the wealth of archaeological information now available to us, and the more we know of the billiant Age of Solomon, the more the question is forced upon us— was he truly wise?

This raises the question: 'What is Wisdom?' The Bible tells us that 'the fear of Yahweh is the beginning of wisdom', and by that phrase means not only a profound respect for God, but also a practical regard for those values of sobriety, industry, generosity, and integrity whereby that reverence for God evinces itself in upright daily living. It would be foolish for us to condemn Solomon for his polygamy, though there as elsewhere he seems to have displayed the same character of flamboyant excess as in other areas of life. Nor should we make too much of his grave errors as a ruler; all men make mistakes, and great men must be expected to make great mistakes. A man may be wise and yet make great mistakes. What we must evaluate is what we may call the general tenor of his life, the distant goals at which he was aiming. Was he setting out to become one more of those dreary oriental despots, who gratified their appetites and especially their lust for power with complete disregard for everyone but themselves? Was his inheritance from David 'my kingdom, my people'? Or was it 'God's Kingdom, God's People, of which I Solomon am the servant' (1 Kings 12: 7)? If it was the former, then King Solomon was a fool. The Bible has a great deal to say about fools, especially in the Book of Proverbs, and Jesus spoke of them also. The Rich Fool was the man who thought that his many goods could fully satisfy him. But if at times it was the latter, if momentarily Solomon caught glimpses of his kingdom and his people as instruments of God's will, co-operating with Him to work out His purposes in history, then he had in some measure the gift of wisdom and the Temple is what we should most remember him by.

'My mind to me a Kingdom is.' It is not for us to be kings in Jerusalem or elsewhere, nor to command vast economic forces, nor to erect great buildings. But to each of us his sovereign kingdom is given, and as King Solomon comes under the judgment of history, so we, too, will one day be judged as to what we have made of that which was given to us. As we try to assess the significance of Solomon and recognize that it is not the judgment of history so much as the judgment of God which is determinative, we may recall those other words we have heard so often: 'Judge therefore yourselves, brethren, that ye be not judged of the Lord.'

ELIJAH

And behold, Yahweh passed by, and a great and strong wind rent the mountains, and broke in pieces the rocks before Yahweh, but Yahweh was not in the wind; and after the wind an earthquake, but Yahweh was not in the earthquake; and after the earthquake a fire, but Yahweh was not in the fire; and after the fire a still, small voice. And when Elijah heard it, he wrapped his face in his mantle and went out and stood at the entrance of the cave.

On the mount of transfiguration, there appeared together with the Christ, Moses and Elijah, the great representatives respectively of the Law and the Prophets. Few would challenge the presence of Moses, but why Elijah? Surely, if one representative prophetic figure is to be singled out, that choice must fall on Isaiah of Jerusalem. His book has been more treasured, studied, quoted, in every age, than all the other prophetic collections put together. Why then Elijah on the mount of transfiguration?

Old Testament prophecy has two major presentations. The first began with the penetration of prophetism into Israel's religion around the eleventh century B.C., in the time of the Judges, and lasted characteristically until the eighth, though it lingered on less prominently and less creditably for long centuries after. The second began in the eighth century with the emergence of a new type of prophet in the persons of Amos and Hosea and lasted until shortly after the Exile when it lapsed far more quickly and decisively than did the former manifestation, which indeed outlived it. The two manifestations of prophecy were thus contemporaneous, with the older form persisting over a considerable period and the newer form dominant during a much shorter period, which ended some two or three hundred years before the other form also petered out.[38] Modern scholars are so impressed

[38] Actually, it is doubtful whether this type of prophetism ever comes to an end—it changes forms and becomes in different ages and cultures apocalypticism, montanism, anabaptism, pentecostalism in turn.

137

—and rightly so—with the great tradition of the so-called 'canonical' prophets, Amos, Isaiah, Jeremiah, Ezekiel, right on to Malachi, that they hardly remember that in fact these were nonconformists to the general tradition; and that the type of prophetism of which Samuel, Nathan, Ahijah, Micaiah are representative was the more normal and usual presentation. When the ancient Hebrews heard the word 'prophet' it was not of men like Micah or Isaiah that they first thought, but of people like 'the man of God' who occurs so often and so anonymously in the Book of Kings. Even Josiah, needing Yahweh's word of decision concerning the book found in the Temple, sent not to Zephaniah or Jeremiah but to 'Huldah the prophetess, wife of Shallum ben Tikvah ben Hashas, keeper of the wardrobe'. The canonical prophets have become far greater in history than they were in contemporary society; prophecy as a current institution was thus most characteristically represented by the striking figure of Elijah. He was the greatest of the exponents of the older type prophetism, and because this was in fact the original, more authentic form not even Isaiah ever displaced him as 'the' prophet. In Malachi we find that the great summoner to repentance before the eschatological day is to be 'the prophet Elijah'. Jesus, himself mistaken by some for Elijah *redivivus*, says that John the Baptist has in fact fulfilled Elijah's rôle, and at a modern Jewish Passover, a place is set for Elijah, in case this year he should come. When the representatives of the Law and the Prophets appeared with the Christ on the mount of transfiguration, it was indeed fitting and appropriate that the disciples should see on the one hand Moses and on the other hand Elijah.

Something of the character of the older type of prophecy emerges from a consideration of the materials offered us by the Book of Kings as the sources for our knowledge of Elijah. There are no oracles of the prophet. We get indeed his conversations reported in direct speech, but we have no confidence that these are anything more than the gist of what he said given in the story-teller's words rather than his own. The preservation of a prophet's own words in his original verse-oracles was dependent on the emergence of a body of disciples, who looked on the prophet as master, and who became over several generations a continuing body, pledged to secure the persistence of their master's teaching. Amos, Hosea, Isaiah were men of such stature and personality that they attracted such a group to themselves, and we may guess that such groups later merged and became interested in more than one prophet. They compiled the small collections of their masters' sayings, which later found their way into writing and were finally caught up into the four great prophetic anthologies 'Isaiah', 'Jeremiah', 'Ezekiel' and 'The Twelve'. But Elijah and those before him, and many after him, had no such close disciple group. They had the vague support of the prophetic movement in general, but this was a very amorphous entity. In most of the stories Elijah is alone, a solitary figure who appears suddenly and disappears with equal rapidity. We do hear of a servant, but he is clearly a mere convenience, and we get neither a glimpse of him nor his name. Rather the activities of Elijah were a favourite subject of the widespread prophetic-minded groups, and tales of his doings were often heard in their fireside talk, and it is these piecemeal traditions which have come down to us. But we have no words of his own. If Amos, Hosea, Micah, Isaiah, are 'written' prophets, and Jeremiah, Ezekiel and Deutero-Isaiah are 'writing' prophets, Elijah and all before him and many after him are indeed 'unwritten' prophets.

The stories have been brought into some consistency by the deuteronomic compilers of the Book of Kings (1 Kings 17–2 Kings 2). They could not give us any background to Elijah, since they possessed none, so he appears suddenly on the stage of history as announcing a fearful drought. It is an interesting point that though in theory he is only the announcer of divine intentions, his personal involvement is such that he is regarded as being to a certain degree responsible for the drought, and if King Ahab could only find him, he would pay dearly for his temerity. Then follow three separate short tales—the feeding of Elijah by ravens at the brook Cherith, the widow's cruse of oil, and the revivification of her son. The first depicts Elijah as under an especial providence of Yahweh; the second emphasizes his dignity and status ('first make me a little cake of it and bring it to me; and afterward make for yourself and your son') and the third stresses the power of Elijah—he brings back the child's life. They are therefore three good stories to let the reader know that this man Elijah is a very remarkable man. Thus the stage is set for the major pieces, the story of the contest on Carmel, and the tremendous narrative of Elijah's experience on Horeb. But the editors had not only Elijah-material for Ahab's reign, but also some relating to 'a man of God' who denounced Ahab for not devoting Benhadad and his people to slaughter; and again a fine narrative concerning Micaiah ben

Imlah's prophecy of Ahab's death. These must find a place in the narrative of Ahab's reign alongside the Elijah material. After the two major narratives of Carmel and Horeb, therefore, the editors insert the Benhadad incident. They then return to their Elijah material for the Naboth story and follow this again with the Micaiah tale and the account of Ahab's death. They also have a story concerning Elijah and Amaziah, Ahab's son, so that goes in next, before the story of his ascension brings the Elijah saga to a close.

There are one or two comments to be made about the selection and arrangement of these materials. The inclusion of the Benhadad story and of the Micaiah ben Imlah incident are both valuable because they reduce Elijah to normal size by reminding us that he was not by any means the only prophet in Israel in Ahab's time. We ourselves would want to move the Naboth incident into the earlier setting of the drought years, where it undoubtedly belongs, and we certainly would have chosen to include some mention of the great battle of Karkar, when Ahab and Benhadad and others beat off a determined Assyrian attack. It is ironic that we know of Ahab's finest hour only from Assyrian records, but then the deuteronomic editors of Kings were strongly averse to showing him in a good light. We would on the other hand have dispensed with the unedifying story from Amaziah's reign, in which the man of God destroys a hundred men and their captains apparently simply to show that he could do it. Its only purpose in the whole pastiche is to re-emphasize the dignity and authority of Elijah, but it does so at a costly expense to his moral stature. On the whole, however, the editors performed well a difficult task in taking a number of separate stories and giving them the appearance of a connected narrative.

Our present interest is to attempt to see Elijah the man. Since we have no words of his own to weigh, we must see him at second hand, reflected in other men's opinions of him. The first three stories and the Amaziah tale are clearly legendary, and we may note them as testifying forcefully to the dynamism of Elijah's character, but we need not linger with them. We shall have more than enough material to consider in the four major narratives—those of Carmel, Horeb, Naboth and the ascension. Just because we do see him only at second hand, we are thereby released from the obligation to sort out the historical Elijah from the deuteronomic Elijah, as we tried to do in the case of Samuel. There we had two major sources, and we could use one to assess the other, and we could distinguish with some clarity between the historical Samuel and the Samuel the deuteronomic compilers wanted us to see. In the case of Elijah, the stories come uniformly from an oral prophetic tradition which has already stylized the man, and all the editors have to do is to give him an additional touch or two of deuteronomic orthodoxy and pass him on to us much as they received him. But it is well to remember that when we remove those touches we do not get back to the historical Elijah, but only to the legend he had become in the prophetic circles. And yet real solid history is never far away—no further than Ahab and Jezebel.

Ahab, as we have already seen, gets a very bad press from the deuteronomic editors of Kings. If, as is probable, Psalm 45 is an epithalamium for the occa-

sion of his marriage to Jezebel, some Hebrews saw him
in a very different light:

> You are the fairest of the sons of men;
>> grace is poured upon your lips;
>> therefore God has blessed you for ever . . .
>> you love righteousness and hate wickedness,
> Therefore God, your God, has annointed you
>> with the oil of gladness above your fellows . . .

Certainly the man who led two thousand chariots into
battle at Karkar and forced an Assyrian army to
retreat was no weakling, and the mortally wounded
king who swayed all day in his jolting chariot lest his
men should see him fall, and finally died of sheer loss
of blood, was something very near a hero. As for
Jezebel, she is the classic instance of a very remarkable
character whose reputation is constantly denigrated
because she happened to be on the wrong side in the
great struggle. Even so, not all the theological prejudice of the compilers of the Book of Kings can rob
her of her courage and strength of purpose. When all
Israel is bedazzled by the brilliance of Elijah's victory
on Carmel, she alone does not lose her head, and reminds him that he has only achieved a nine days'
wonder and that when all the excitement has died
down he will be at her mercy: 'so may the gods do
to me, and more also, if I do not make your life as the
life of one of them by this time tomorrow'. And the
story of her sheer heroism in the face of Jehu's ruthless
brutality cannot but arouse our enthusiasm. Had she
only been for Yahweh rather than against him, her
name would have been as honoured as it is now a
byword of infamy.

The point at issue between these three is a serious

143

one. It is a theological issue, as well as a cultural and political one. Was Israel to be modernized, to be brought up to date, to be drawn into the cultural and political progress of the civilization of the Fertile Crescent, or was it to remain an uncouth, barbaric backwater, unstirred by the rising tides of power politics and material advance? My own guess is that Jezebel was a woman with a mission—to spread the light of Phoenician civilization into the backward hill-state into which she had been thrown by the mere chance of a political marriage. Her tragedy was that she could not recognize the theological problem involved. It seemed to her but a small thing that Israel must pay for the advantages of being drawn into the community of nations the price of a syncretism of her national Yahwism with the prevailing Baalism of her neighbours. Yet from our vantage point of history we can see that it would in fact have been the end of Israel. All her pomp of yesterday would literally have been one with Nineveh and Tyre, and robbed of her distinctive character she would have sunk into complete obscurity as a Phoenician dependency, from which even modern scholarship would probably not have bothered to resurrect her. Israel would have meant to subsequent history no more than has Edom or Moab. Elijah, on the other hand, did recognize that. He saw that Yahweh and Israel must stay together. If the bonds of covenant forged by Moses were once broken, then Israel had no further destiny or significance. He moves therefore into a fierce and unrelenting opposition to Jezebel.

The first clash, however, had the character of a preliminary skirmish. Ahab desired the vineyard of Naboth, and Jezebel devised a scheme to procure it.

Presumably the drought which befell the country during Ahab's reign had already begun to make wretched the lives of the peasants, so Jezebel had a fast proclaimed in Naboth's village and secured his elevation as the leader of the ceremonies of prostration, clothes-rending, dust-throwing, and other (to our mind) extravagant demonstrations of grief which accompanied the laments on such occasions. Just when emotions were running high and the starving peasants were at an inflammable point of excitement, her agents supplied the spark. 'Why has this drought come? We can tell you! That hypocrite Naboth, so piously leading our laments, is in fact the cause of all our misery! We heard him! We heard him curse God and the King!' Jezebel's psychological intuition served her well. First you raise a nonentity to a position of eminence, thus arousing subconscious resentment and jealousies, and then suddenly you offer him as a scapegoat to receive the general animosities of the people. Blinded by desperation and hysterical with hunger, the mob fell on Naboth and the ugly passions of a lynch-mob found their terrible catharsis. Of course, next day when the reaction set in and they saw Ahab taking over their old neighbour's freeholding, they realized they had been tricked and manipulated. But it was only Elijah who had the courage to put the general sentiment into words: 'Have you killed, and also taken possession? In the place where dogs licked up the blood of Naboth shall dogs lick your own blood!' It was probably shortly afterwards that Elijah announced a different interpretation of the drought: it was, he said, a clear sign of the fearsome anger of Yahweh at the policies of Ahab and of the power behind Ahab, the Phoenician princess Jezebel.

145

Thus was war declared between the royal house and the prophetic movement. Some of the more noisy and outspoken adherents of the movement were rounded up and put to death for treason, and Elijah himself found it expedient to disappear. The drought dragged slowly on, even into the third rainy season, and still there was no sign of release. Then Elijah emerged and demanded a trial by ordeal—let the deity who answered by fire be recognized as God of Israel! When the lightning struck on Carmel giving Elijah his victory, he promised rain, and as it began to fall Ahab had to submit to the final indignity of having Elijah as his outrunner all the way back to Jezreel, shouting as he ran: 'Yahweh is God!' What really happened on Carmel? We cannot tell. If you believe in miracles, you will answer 'a miracle'. If you like pseudo-scientific explanations you may reply 'lightning struck by a happy coincidence', but if you have a regard for human nature you will say that something extraordinary took place which swung the fickle mob on to Elijah's side. For the moment they were his, and Ahab and Jezebel were rendered powerless. The poor wretches of Baal-fanatics fell as readily prey to the lynch-mob as had Naboth, and Elijah was in all things triumphant. A new set of victims for the sullen fury of a crazed mob had been found and the prophet rode the crest of popular support. Then came Jezebel's message, and all Elijah's elation oozed away through the gaping hole she had made in his self-esteem. How right she was! How easily she could turn the mob against him! Naboth—the prophets of Baal—himself the next victim! He turned and ran for his life into the safety and the despair of the desert. From beneath the juniper bush rose a despairing cry: 'Now, Yahweh, take away my life, for I am no better than my fathers!' Moses, Joshua, Samuel—they all tried with this people and they all failed—and now Elijah also.

So he came to Sinai-Horeb[39] where the great experiment of covenant between Yahweh and Israel first began. Here it began and here it was fittingly to end. The covenant was dissolved and one man had returned to report the apostasy of a nation. But where Elijah came to write 'finis' to the whole wretched story, he discovered, as men so often do discover, that man's ends are God's beginnings: 'Go, return on your way to the wilderness of Damascus; and when you arrive, you shall anoint Hazael to be king over Syria; and Jehu, the son of Nimshi you shall anoint to be king of Israel; and Elisha, the son of Shaphat of Abelmeholah, you shall anoint to be prophet in your place' (1 Kings 19: 15–16). Yahweh was *not* finished with Israel. He had the next moves planned—and dread moves they were. Syria was to become the scourge of Israel, who was to learn afresh in bitter warfare her dependence on Yahweh. Even more severe would be the purging of the nation by a new fanatic king of her own, Jehu the ruthless butcher. But beyond these two lay a third grim ordeal, the constant discipline of Yahweh, announced and made effective by the prophetic order, symbolized by his own successor, Elisha. Only out of these fierce fires of disaster and suffering could a purified, sober and loyal Israel emerge. 'Him who escapes the sword of Hazael shall Jehu slay, and him who escapes from the sword of Jehu shall Elisha slay; yet I will leave seven thousand in Israel, all the knees that

[39] The compilers probably accepted the identification of 'Horeb' and 'Sinai', though they continued to use the Northern Israelite name 'Horeb' for the location of the institution of the Mosaic covenant.

have not bowed to Baal and every mouth that has not kissed him.'

How much of this is Elijah's own thinking? When he meditated in that lonely cave on Horeb, how much of the ways of God were revealed to him? Or is this only the *post hoc propter hoc* theology of the deuteronomic compilers of the Book of Kings? The symbolism of the passage is strikingly clear—the violence of the storm answers to the violence of the mob through which Elijah had sought to work his will on Israel—but Yahweh was not in the wind, nor the fire, nor even the shuddering earthquake, just as he was not in the tempestuous emotions of an Israelite mob. But he is in the long, steady movement of history, the slow outworking of events, and the unfolding processes of moral judgment on nations and men alike, which are understood only in retrospect, and in quiet reflection, and in the silence which speaks to the heart. It is when men hear that, that they wrap their face in their mantle and know that they stand before the Lord.

As we look back and survey again the Elijah narratives we wonder that the same compilers could include (and probably be largely responsible for) the high drama of the scene on Carmel and the searching insights of the Horeb narrative and then also throw in the childlike stories of the ravens and the cruse of oil, and even not flinch from adding the absurdity of the Amaziah episode. It is, however, a reminder to us that religious insights—or the lack of them—can be revealed at many levels of understanding, from the naïve to the deeply thoughtful, from the story of the Garden of Eden to the majestic periods of Second

Isaiah, from the prophetic traditions of Elijah to the philosophic questionings of Job. The Bible is not a level book, uniformly inspired, but has many a dim trough and many a lofty peak. As we read, we need the guidance of the Holy Spirit, to help us distinguish the one from the other.

With regard to Elijah himself, we are often aware that we are at one remove from history. We know that we walk firm ground as we meet Ahab and Jezebel, but by the brook Cherith we are treading in the path of legend, while on Carmel and particularly on Horeb we are conscious that this holy ground is history theologized. The Elijah of history is, in fact, hidden from us by the overlay of legend and of deuteronomic theology, and yet perhaps at one point legend, theology, and history come fittingly together. For as Elijah ascends in the whirlwind, we see the fiery chariot symbolizing that medium of legend which here, as elsewhere in the Old Testament, is the vehicle of so much that is profound; and as the mantle of Elijah falls on Elisha, we remember that the continuing line of prophets, who can interpret the events of their day as activities of the will of God, is living theology in action; and when we recall that that same prophetic movement instigated the revolt which overthrew the house of Omri and brought Jehu to the throne, and thus occasioned all the dire political consequences of that event, we are reminded that it is in history and not in doctrine that the revelation of God is made known. And though we may not see very clearly the historical person of Elijah himself, nevertheless the rôle of the prophet as interpreter of the significance of contemporary history is so exemplified in him, that it is indeed fitting that of all the

L

prophets he should stand with Moses on the Mount of Transfiguration and confer with the Christ concerning his approaching death.

ISAIAH

In that day the Lord Yahweh of hosts
    called to weeping and mourning,
    to baldness and girding with sackcloth;
and behold joy and gladness,
    slaying oxen and killing sheep,
    eating flesh and drinking wine.
'Let us eat and drink,
    for tomorrow we die.'
Yahweh of hosts has revealed himself in my ears;
'Surely this iniquity will not be forgiven you
    till you die,'
    says the Lord Yahweh of hosts.

Before we can discuss the man, we must pronounce upon the book, and the first thing to be said about the book is that it is not a book. As instructed by the White Rabbit, we expect a book to begin at the beginning, to go through to the end and stop. A book introduces its subject, develops it, draws conclusions and finally indicates its further reference, all in an orderly and rational fashion. The so-called Book of Isaiah, however, plunges *in medias res* with its second verse, continues on no coherent or discernible plan for sixty-six chapters, when it breaks off as abruptly as it began. In fact, it is not a book but an anthology, and an ill-arranged one at that.

Nevertheless, in this strange assortment of jumbled pieces there are to be found the most striking, the most lofty, the most noble utterances of the Hebrew prophetic movement, from the eighth to the third centuries before Christ. Consequently, it has been more closely studied than any other of the Four Scrolls of the Prophets. It was in this scroll that Jesus looked in the synagogue at Nazareth for the programme of His mission; it is this scroll which is most often quoted by the New Testament writers; it is this prophetic work which was most frequently copied at Qumran; and the shelves of any modern theological library will reveal almost as much written on Isaiah as on all the rest of the prophets put together.

Not everything in the anthology which bears his name is Isaiah's own work. He inspired a movement

153

which continued its concern into centuries long after
his own. But the small opening collections of oracles,
Chapters 1, 2–4, 5, 6–12, are generally reckoned as
being Isaianic in the main, as are also Chapters 28–31.
Certainly, here is rich enough material and to spare,
upon which to draw for our portrait of the man. Our
problem will still be that of choosing what is superlative
as compared with what is good, and in deciding which
aspect of his many-sided character we should attempt
to display. For his personality is as complex as the
structure of his book, and as it outranks all other prophetic collections, so the man is pre-eminent among
the great men of his age. I am, however, going to
concentrate on what I conceive to be his major rôle.

It is always tempting to draw parallels between some
bygone era and our own times. Professor Arnold
Toynbee has remarkably illustrated both the attrac-
tiveness and the peril of doing so. But the political
situation of Isaiah's time and that of today are, viewed
with some objectivity, not unalike. An old and relatively stable political order was being threatened by
new and largely unknown forces. The distinctiveness
of Israel as springing from her religion and the sense
of being different from other peoples, which went back
to the days of the amphictyonic covenant, were in
danger of being lost by her absorption into the cosmopolitan maw of the Assyrian empire. The Royal House,
which had maintained itself in Judah for nearly two
hundred years and was one of the few constants in the
political kaleidoscope, seemed likely to be swept away
in the same manner as the upstart kings of Northern
Israel were disappearing, one after the other. The
Temple, that unique and most holy shrine, which

more than anything else symbolized the permanence and stability of Judah's providential existence, lay itself in the path of invading armies. The old order, represented to the young Isaiah by the forty-year reigns of Jeroboam in the North, and of Uzziah in the South, was clearly passing, but what the new age would hold, none could foresee. It is significant, therefore, that Isaiah dated his call to the prophetic ministry as being 'in the year that king Uzziah died' (6: 1). It bespeaks from the beginning his political interest.

As he began, so he continued. From 742 through to 701 or (if John Bright is correct in assuming a second invasion by Sennacherib) right on to 688, Isaiah took a close, continual, and lively interest in politics. Nor was he afraid of taking a partisan viewpoint and holding to it; he was quite the John Collins or Donald Soper of his times. The great question of the day was Judah's attitude to Assyria. Should she 'collaborate'— an eager submission before it was called for, a toadying offer of military support, a sycophantic adoption of Assyrian language, fashions and cults? Or should she 'resist'—organizing a coalition of small states, fomenting rebellions elsewhere in the Assyrian empire, entering into clandestine plots with Egypt on the promise of arms and men? Which path should she take? The Judean court was sharply divided, but Isaiah saw the perils of both policies. For any reliance on Egypt he had only the utmost, unmitigated scorn: she would prove a broken reed to anyone leaning upon her, her nickname 'Rahab' (the restless one) would be demonstrated by a masterly inactivity, and the net result of looking to her for help would be shame and humiliation. To drive the lesson home, he went about Jerusalem stripped to a loincloth and barefoot for some three years, illustrating the way the Egyptians would be marched north to Nineveh when the Assyrians conquered them. To covenant with Egypt, he asserted, was to covenant with death, and to trust in her promises was to trust in lies and deceit.[40] Towards Assyria, however, his attitude was more complex. Judah, he held, should clearly do nothing to attract Assyria's attention. He was strongly opposed to Ahaz, for example, when the latter appealed to Tiglath-Pilezer III for help against the combined Syrian-Israelite invasion in 736. On the other hand, he saw that sooner or later an Assyrian invasion was inevitable and he believed that Judah should accept it without resistance, as a punishment laid on the nation by a disciplining God. Much that was lovely and desirable would be lost, and there would be cruel suffering and bitter shame, but from the experience would emerge a chastened and purified remnant of the sacred nation (Isaiah 10: 20–23). But when the Assyrians overran the country, pillaging, looting, murdering, Isaiah was moved so deeply as to change his stand and to urge Hezekiah to be firm in resistance. Jerusalem at least, he proclaimed, should remain inviolate. The Assyrians had maliciously overplayed their rôle, and they would therefore receive from Yahweh a fearful recompense of destruction and overthrow.[41] Isaiah's was always a bold policy, bold in the face of patriotic fervour in urging non-resistance, and equally bold in urging stout-hearted defiance in the face of an apparently irresistible enemy.

But while it can readily be shown that Isaiah had very definite views with regard to the burning political

[40] Isa. 30: 1–5; 6–7; 31: 1–3; 20: 1–6; 28: 14–22.
[41] Isa. 10: 24–27. Cf. especially 37: 21–32.

questions of his day, the determinant element in his thinking, which was responsible for those views, is not so easily exposed. As so often happens in biographical studies, the political views and attitudes to which the inner principle gives rise, are readily distinguishable and frequently expressed, while the inner principle is by the subject himself mostly taken for granted or only tacitly assumed. Not many men are given to self-analysis and track down within themselves the operative motive and the dominant persuasion—and certainly not an impetuous, vigorous person, such as Isaiah. We have to sift his words and weigh his actions, and so try to arrive at an understanding of his character and motives.

It is fairly clear that Isaiah saw Israel as the holy, elect, covenant people, whose one duty and destiny it was to maintain utter loyalty to Yahweh and Yahweh only. If Judah would fulfil this calling, she would survive, he believed, all political upheavals and vicissitudes, and emerge from the days of crises a purified, wiser, and more mature people. She must, therefore, avoid all foreign alliances, all political expediencies and all cultural or religious compromises. Her policy must be to keep disentangled politically, in order that she may not be compromised religiously. Thus we get the formulation of Isaiah's basic maxims; 'He who believes will not be in haste', 'In returning and rest you shall be saved, in quietness and in trust shall be your strength', and 'If you will not believe, surely you shall not be established'.[42] Each in its own way expresses Isaiah's dominant conviction that only by utter dependence on her covenant status with Yahweh could Judah hope for any kind of future whatsoever.

[42] Isa. 28: 16; 30: 15; 7: 9.

For Isaiah, as for so many before and since, the religious challenge inherent in the political situation was the challenge to risk Judah's whole future on a series of uncertainties—whether there is a God, whether Israel knows Him adequately, whether her teachers have interpreted His words accurately, whether His will is that Judah should be saved. If there were a mistake involved in any one of those propositions, then Judah should at once initiate negotiations with Assyria, and get herself on the side of the big battalions as quickly as possible. But if those propositions were sound, as Isaiah believed they were, then she must keep out of all entanglements and steadfastly refuse to play the dangerous game of power-politics. It was Isaiah's profound conviction that if Judah was true to her covenant loyalty, Assyria would not be allowed to destroy her, even if it should take a miracle to save her.

The preacher who takes sides politically thereby forfeits the protection afforded by the unwritten but almost universally recognized rule that 'the cloth' is never overtly attacked—at least, not by gentlemen. Probably this immunity is afforded partly because the clergy are thought to be ornamental, anachronistic, and irrelevant, and partly also to ensure that they shall remain so. It is the cast of mind which goes with the cry 'let's keep politics out of religion'—meaning, of course, 'let's keep religion out of politics'.

Isaiah would have agreed with neither proposition and certainly did not expect or obtain any immunity from sharp criticism. The pro-Egyptian party accused him of imagining you could run a government as if it were a Sunday School, and of going around telling everybody what should be done, as if he were the teacher and all others were children in the kindergarten (28: 9–10). Others grew tired of his threatening them with the judgment of God and told Isaiah that he had better hurry up and produce this mighty judgment, if he wanted them to believe it (5: 18–19). Isaiah did not accept such criticism without hitting back. He accused the nobles of profligacy, corruption, and deliberate self-deception; they were such men as those

> who say to the seers 'See not';
>   and to the prophets: 'Prophesy not to us what is right,
> speak to us smooth things, prophesy illusions,
> leave the way, turn aside from the path,
>   let us hear no more of the Holy One of Israel.'
>   (30: 10–11)

It was because of this diseased readiness to 'call evil good, and good evil, to put darkness for light and light for darkness, to put sweet for bitter and bitter for sweet' that Isaiah believed that only a fearful cauterizing could burn Judah clean of these irrational and destructive perversities. He would have well understood Scott Holland's prayer: 'With Thy living fire of judgement, Purge this realm of bitter things'. There was, he knew, something unhealthy, abhorrent, deepseated like a cancer, eating at Judah's moral fibre, and only the most radical surgery could effect a cure. And yet because Yahweh was the God of righteousness and of a moral holiness which could sear and burn, Isaiah hoped as confidently for the miracle of spiritual renewal as he expected the miracle of physical salvation:

How the faithful city
  has become a harlot,
  she that was full of justice!
Righteousness lodged in her,
  but now murderers. . . .
I will turn my hand against you
  and will smelt away your dross as with lye,
  and remove all your alloy.
And I will restore your judges as at the first,
  and your counselors as at the beginning.
Afterward you shall be called the city of righteousness,
  the faithful city.   (1 : 21, 25, 26)

The tragedy of Isaiah's ministry arose from the fact that he experienced the one miracle and was denied the other. He prophesied the city would not be taken, and at the very last moment 'the angel of death' intervened to smite the Assyrian army with such losses by plague that it was forced to withdraw, and the city escaped capture by the very narrowest hair's breadth. The land was ravaged and torn, and Judah left bruised and bleeding but alive. By divine intervention she had been wonderfully snatched from the very brink of destruction. The living fire of judgment had indeed burned through Judah, and now the prophet looked to see the nation, purged and cleansed, return in penitence to a forgiving God. But miracles of physical salvation are easier to come by than miracles of spiritual renewal. There was in fact no change of heart. The people were as stupid, insensitive, and perverse as they were before the Assyrian invasion. The surgery had gone deep and had cured nothing. As Isaiah looked down from the roof-top on the delirious crowds mafficking in the streets, there welled up out of his heart a last judgment on the whole nation:

In that day the Lord Yahweh of hosts,
   called to weeping and mourning,
   to baldness and girding with sackcloth;

and behold, joy and gladness,
   slaying oxen and killing sheep,
   eating flesh and drinking wine.
'Let us eat and drink, for tomorrow we die.'

Yahweh of hosts has revealed himself in my ears:
'Surely this iniquity will not be forgiven you till you die,'
   says the Lord Yahweh of hosts.

(22: 12–14)

If it was in the year 701 that the invasion and deliverance occurred Isaiah was already an old man; if in 688, he was indeed aged. We may think it was not long after, perhaps in his very last days, that he shared with his little disciple band his attempt to understand what had happened to him (6: 1–13). He remembered how it all began, away back 'in the year that king Uzziah died'. He remembered the call and how eagerly he had offered 'Here am I. Send me!' He had not known it then, but now looking back, it all became heart-breakingly clear. He had thought then, in his youthful optimism, that he was being sent to preach salvation and redemption to those people; yes, and he had gone on thinking, all his ministry, that that was what he was doing—but now, in these last days, it had all become plain: he had been sent not to preach for Judah's conversion but for her destruction. It was his preaching which was to harden her heart, deaden her conscience, and make her a dumb brute, fit only for the slaughterer:

> And he said: 'Go and say to this people:
>   "Hear and hear, but do not understand;
>   see and see, but do not perceive."
> Make the heart of this people fat,
>   and their ears heavy,
>   and shut their eyes,
> lest they see with their eyes, and hear with their ears,
>   and understand with their hearts, and turn and be
>   healed.'

But how long was this to go on? Would not the other and greater miracle follow upon the lesser? After physical salvation, would there not come spiritual renewal? With the wisdom of old age he now knew what the answer was. It was the word that had been given to Amos, his forerunner, the man from whom he had learnt so much. He now knew that his message and that of Amos were the same, a message of doom on a guilty people.

> Then I said: 'How long, O Lord?'
> And he said: 'Until cities lie waste without inhabitant,
>   and houses without men, and the land is utterly
>   desolate,
> And Yahweh removes men far away,
>   and the forsaken places are many in the midst of the
>   land.'[43]

Isaiah died convinced of the failure of his mission to Judah.

As we look back from our vantage point of twenty-five centuries, we realize that a death-bed is a small eminence from which to make more than a hasty judgment on any life. Isaiah, we can see, was wrong.

[43] Isa. 6: 11–12. Cf. Amos 7: 1–9.

When he came to the conclusion that his ministry had only hardened Judah's heart and that this was what God must have planned from the beginning, he was quite, quite wrong. It may be that we shall be reminded that we too are not likely to come to a true assessment of our own endeavour.

It may be also that we shall ponder another reflection. Isaiah was a political prophet. He was much else besides, and with those other aspects of his many-sided ministry, I have not dealt. But first and foremost he was a political prophet, and he thought that through political events the Kingdom of God would come. But it takes more than wars and bombings and Dunkirks and battles of Britain and Pearl Harbours and Hiroshimas, to effect a moral change in the human heart. Elijah learnt under a juniper tree that Mount Carmel miracles count in fact for very little, but Isaiah never quite grasped the same lesson. He still hoped for the Kingdom of God to come through a political event. There are those today who think that a change of economic structure, a new system of government, a sweeping revision of educational systems, will work that second and greater miracle, the change in human willing.

This is not to say that external miracles do not occur. They do. Nor is it to say that they are not desirable. They are. The raising of the siege of Jerusalem was as significant to Judah as El Alamein was to Britain. Social revolution sometimes achieves a very great deal. To gain equality of opportunity for all, to banish poverty, and to outlaw war are our necessary and immediate goals if the human race is to survive. The raising of the siege of Jerusalem was also necessary if Judah was to survive: *but when she survived, she was still what she had always been.* If by a miracle we also survive, that other and greater miracle will still be to come, the miracle which politics cannot begin to achieve—the total renewal of human nature, or, as Ezekiel put it, the taking away of the heart of stone and the implanting of the heart of flesh. We still need to learn the deep meaning of Wesley's line: 'Sin be more than hell abhorred'. It can be learned only at the foot of the cross.

JEREMIAH

But this is the covenant which I will make with the house of Israel after those days, says Yahweh: I will put my law within them, and I will write it upon their hearts; and I will be their God, and they shall be my people. And no longer shall each man teach his neighbor and each his brother, saying: 'Know Yahweh', for they shall all know me, from the least of them to the greatest, says Yahweh.

The Book of the Prophet Jeremiah is both more simple and more complex than that of Isaiah. It is more simple in that the great bulk of its material is Jeremianic—it either originated with him or is concerned with him. On the other hand, it is more complex in that a second figure interposes between us and Jeremiah in the person of his amanuensis and editor Baruch, and we have to allow for the latter's handling of the original material. In the continuing generations of the 'Isaiah Society', the personal idiosyncrasies of any one 'traditionist' were lost in the general influence of the corporate mind; in Baruch's case, he plays Boswell to a Dr. Johnson of whom we have no other record, and he does not indicate when he is simply transcribing Jeremiah, or when he is paraphrasing him, or when he is indulging in a little vicarious plagiarizing on his behalf.

Since a considerable number of the oracles contained in the book are in verse, we may presume them to be the prophet's own words, unless they are clearly anachronistic or wildly out of character—though with a complex person like Jeremiah this last is never a very certain quality. The prose paraphrases of oracles originally in verse, whether transcribed by Jeremiah or Baruch,[44] have a deuteronomic styling which is simply the hall-mark of the age, and indicates nothing

---

[44] Cf. Jer. 36: 4 and 36: 32. Jeremiah was debarred from entering the Temple so he dictated earlier oracles to Baruch, who then read them in the Temple. When the scroll was destroyed, Jeremiah dictated a second one, of which it is remarked 'and many similar words were added to them', probably by Baruch. Cf. also 45: 1–5.

more than that both men had been given a good grounding in the scribal schools. The shorter the version probably the nearer we are to the prophet's own words, but there are no obvious signs in these paraphrases of his message having been misrepresented. The latter part of the book becomes more and more narrative in character, but we observe here also that the Jeremiah depicted is not foreign to the Jeremiah who uttered the verse oracles. On the whole we may, I think, give Baruch high marks for a fair and accurate presentation of his master. Nevertheless, we are on the surest ground when we are handling the oracles preserved in their original verse.

Outstanding among the materials with which the book presents us are the first person narratives, and the private prayers of Jeremiah in which he is speaking directly to God. I once made the mistake of comparing these two kinds of material with Wesley's Journal and Wesley's Diary—the one written for publication, and the other in code, intended for himself and God alone. It is a good example of the mistake arising from applying modern, Western, literary-critical categories to ancient, Eastern folk-literary material. The correction, as Gunkel taught us, can only be reached by resorting to the 'setting in life'. Where and under what conditions was such material likely to be produced?

The fact that the Book of Jeremiah, and the Book of Psalms contain so much that is alike in style and content gives us the clue. The Psalter has two main 'settings in life', the inner and the outer courts of the Temple. From the inner court came the cultic and liturgical compositions while from the outer court came the products of the *ṣodh*. The *ṣodh* or circle was simply a group which met from time to time to converse. In the villages, it was the men of the community in counsel, and legal cases or neighbourhood projects or other matters of general interest came up for discussion and decision. But it was also (very much after the style of a small-town 'weekly') the place of news-dissemination, gossip, the telling of tales, the instruction of the young, and the 'publication' of poetry. Within this last category came the expression of a man's religious experience in prayer or psalm. No doubt the *şodhim* (we may be sure there were several such groups) which gathered in the outer court of the Temple were more given to religious conversations than to secular affairs. Here the man who had been ill expressed his sense of relief and his thanksgiving for recovery; those who felt themselves ostracized, or threatened by personal enemies, poured out their complaints. It was here that a man announced his sense of call to a prophetic ministry and here that prophets uttered oracles to the listening groups. Jeremiah's personal prayers to Yahweh, so reminiscent of the 'individual laments' of the Psalter, were doubtless first heard in the setting of a temple *şodh*. Similarly, the story of his call and his initiatory experiences[45] were probably first given to his *şodh* in a spirited, elevated prose style, which rose in the Yahweh utterances to genuine verse, and were later recorded in more sober prose with only the Yahweh-oracles retaining their original verse-form. Thus a great deal of

---

[45] The true first-person narratives are largely confined to the first chapter of the book; elsewhere we simply get an introductory statement to some of the prose oracles: 'And Yahweh said to me'. The third-person narratives which begin at Chapter 7, and which from Chapter 25 dominate the rest of the book, are presumably the work of Baruch, though he clearly at times provided his third-person introductions to what had originally been included by Jeremiah in his own first-person edition of his messages. The two men may well be said to have collaborated in the book.

the material of this Jeremiah anthology originates
directly from close to the prophet, and we can have a
high confidence in it as a witness to the kind of person
he was.

Owing to this historically dependable and relatively
abundant source of material, the story of Jeremiah's
life can be sketched more fully than that of any other
Old Testament personality, with the sole possible
exception of David. We are told that he came from
a priestly family having its home at Anathoth (1: 1),
and though it has been disputed, there are, I think,
very good reasons for accepting this tradition. At an
early age he believed himself called to a prophetic
ministry, probably being stirred into activity by the
dangers to which Judah was exposed by the collapse
of the Assyrian power after the death of Asshurbanipal.
Jeremiah preached that Judah was to be punished by
Yahweh at the hands of 'the Foe from the North'
(Jer. 4–6). The first result, however, of the weakening
of Assyria was a new freedom for Judah and, under the
leadership of her able and active king Josiah, she began
to nurse hopes of bringing Northern Israel back into
the Davidic kingdom. Thus it seemed that Jeremiah
was shown at the very beginning of his ministry to be
a false prophet, and the more he insisted on the
imminence of disaster, the more people jeered at him.
It was out of this experience, doubly bitter for a young
man, that he produced for his *şodh* one of his most
striking pieces:

> Yahweh, thou hast deceived me,
>   and I was deceived;
> thou art stronger than I,
>   and thou hast prevailed.

I have become a laughingstock all the day;
    everyone mocks me.

For whenever I speak, I cry out,
    I shout: 'Violence and destruction!'
For the word of Yahweh has become for me
    a reproach and derision all day long.

If I say: 'I will not mention him,
    or speak any more in his name,'
there is in my heart as it were a burning fire
    shut up in my bones,
and I am weary with holding it in,
    and I cannot.

For I hear many whispering.
    Terror is on every side!
'Denounce him! Let us denounce him!'
    say all my familiar friends,
    watching for my fall.
'Perhaps he will be deceived,
    then we can overcome him,
    and take our revenge on him.'

Here we are given straightway an insight into his nature—sensitive, quick to feel and to be hurt, passionate and intense. But there is nothing weak or effeminate about him. He is prepared to give back as good as he gets, and he is very far from being the mild, gentle, and forgiving soul the sentimentalists make him out to be:

But Yahweh is with me as a dread warrior;
    therefore my persecutors will stumble,
    they will not overcome me.
They will be greatly shamed,
    for they will not succeed.

> Their eternal dishonor
> will never be forgotten.
>
> O Yahweh of hosts, who triest the righteous,
> who seest the heart and the mind,
> let me see thy vengeance upon them,
> for to thee have I committed my cause.
>
> (20: 7–12)

Characteristically he thought of himself as 'a fortified city, an iron pillar and bronze walls', and though he should be left *Athanasius contra mundum* he would still stand unmoved and unyielding (1: 18–19).

The decay of Assyria and the consequent rise of political hope was inevitably attended by a revival of the national religion, and this presented the opportunity for which a group of reformers had been waiting. Whether they were members of the same movement which had produced the law-book we call Deuteronomy, and deposited it in the temple, or were genuinely surprised to find it there and gave it their allegiance solely because they were impressed by its teaching, we cannot now say. The fact is that this law-book became the platform of Josiah's reforming policy, and the scroll was widely accepted as the final and absolute expression of God's will for Israel. There seems no reason to doubt that Jeremiah was at first thoroughly enthusiastic about the programme and committed himself deeply in its support. We have a reference to a preaching mission advocating adherence to the reform, to which, however, his family were bitterly opposed, so much so that some of his relatives sought to silence him, if necessary by assassination.[46]

[46] Cf. Jer. 11: 18–20 and 11: 21–23. If the family were acting as priests of a local shrine at Anathoth, the deuteronomic innovation of a demand for a single, central sanctuary (Deut. 12: 1–14) would arouse their particular opposition.

Later, however, he became dissatisfied with the shallowness of the thinking of the reform adherents and withdrew his support from the movement. It was not long, however, before political events made the whole reformation programme irrelevant.

Those political events produced the most dramatic change in the whole history of the Judean kingdom. In 610 B.C. her future had never seemed brighter. The king was able, active, and conscientious. He had put himself at the head of a popular movement for reform of the nation's life and the nation's religion, and though there must have been some resentment, he had that virtue of success which disarms opposition. The collapse of Assyria allowed him to assert his country's independence and even to re-occupy a good deal of former Northern Israelite territory. Men began to dream of the return of the old Davidic days. Two years later that hope had passed away forever. Pharaoh Necho marched north through Palestine, apparently to Assyria's aid, and Josiah, with splendid courage and doubtless relying on divine aid, tried to hold the pass at Megiddo. Whether his idea was simply to preserve his independence, or whether he hoped to delay Egypt and thus ensure the end of Assyria, we shall never know. We are not even sure if there was a battle or whether there was merely some kind of a court martial.[47] The assured facts are that there was no divine intervention, and that Josiah died at Megiddo, and that the political hopes of Judah died with him. First Egypt, and then on her defeat, Babylon claimed suzerainty over Judah. Revolts in 597 and 587 ended in mass deportations, and the complete destruction of

Public support of the programme by a young member of their own family (11: 1–6) would naturally anger them greatly.

[47] 2 Chron. 35: 20–27 describes a battle, but 2 Kings 23: 29 is deliberately vague.

173

Judah as a state and of Jerusalem as a city. There can be no programme of reform in a kingdom which no longer exists.

During this period, Jeremiah's preoccupation was very naturally with these political upheavals. He is silent on the tragedy of Josiah's death, which probably means that like the rest of his contemporaries he was baffled by the lack of divine intervention. It is significant that no one in the Old Testament cares to comment on the king's fate. By all the rules, godly and zealous as he was, Josiah had every right to expect providential protection, and it had been conspicuously absent. The only explanation men could make was to throw the blame on the sins of his predecessors—'the fathers have eaten sour grapes and the children's teeth are set on edge'—and try to forget the whole miserable business. On the kings who followed Josiah, however, Jeremiah is by no means silent. He laments over Shallum (Jehoahaz) because he will never return from captivity in Egypt, and he prophesies that Coniah (Jehoiachin) will similarly die in Babylon. For Jehoiakim, who ruled for some ten years between these two short reigns, he had nothing but contempt. As for Zedekiah, the last king of all, Jeremiah could only look to the time when the Messiah would come and would truly deserve the name to which Zedekiah ('Yahweh is my Righteousness') so conspicuously failed to respond.[48]

As the disaster threatening Judah drew ever nearer, Jeremiah's political message became more definite and more uncompromising—'Submit to the Babylonians'. In the uneasy years between the two deportations he warned the exiles already in Babylon to settle down

[48] Jer. 22: 10–12 and 28–30; 22: 13–19 and 23: 5–6.

and prepare for a stay of at least two generations, and when the final fighting broke out in Jerusalem, he persistently urged surrender. Like Isaiah before him, he construed the invasion as a divine chastisement which must be received with meekness and penitence. It was this apparently defeatist attitude which earned him the hatred of the militarists and nearly cost him his life at their hands (37: 11–38: 13).

When the city fell, the Babylonians also assumed that Jeremiah had been a 'fifth columnist' on their behalf and sought to reward him. He, however, asked merely to remain in Judah, and thus he became involved in the squalid events of Gedaliah's assassination, and the final ignoble flight to Egypt. It was here that he had his last prophetic encounter. The Jewish exiles were, he discovered, worshipping the Queen of Heaven. Jeremiah was aghast—had not all the disasters that had befallen them cured them forever of such idolatries? But the womenfolk waved him impatiently on one side; in the old days they had worshipped the Queen of Heaven and all had been well with them. Then came the reform of religion in Yahweh's name and nothing had been right ever since. So they were not going to bother with Yahweh any more, but were going to return to the Mother whom they could trust and whom they should never have forsaken (44: 15–19). Jeremiah discovered in his old age that the prophetic interpretation of history is all a matter of a point of view. As far as we know, he died soon after in exile in Egypt. He cannot have been a happy man.

Jeremiah is not remembered primarily as a political prophet. True he conceived of his own rôle in terms of what we should now call 'an international affairs expert' (1 : 9), but he was neither the first nor the last man who did not recognize wherein his own true greatness lay. In so far as he urged submission to Babylon, he was in the tradition of Isaiah and the eighth-century prophets in general, but in fact it was the only practical policy left. Egypt was a broken reed. Depending on divine miracle had proved disastrous for the godly Josiah, and there was certainly no reason to think it would prove any more helpful for miserable little Zedekiah. The only course left was to submit to Babylon, and it hardly required a major prophet to say so.

Where the prophetic character of Jeremiah's vision did show itself, however, was in his belief that despite all the disasters, Judah would one day revive and the people of God would continue. This was the real issue between him and the housewives in Egypt. For the immediate prosperity of their families, the safety of their children, and the very lives of their menfolk, they preferred to trust the Queen of Heaven—the long perspectives of history did not concern them. But because Jeremiah knew that Israel was God's elected instrument in history, he saw that these present troubles must be but incidents in the long, unfolding story which would continue into time, far beyond his own day. That is why he bought the apparently worthless field at Anathoth and also why he elected to stay in the ravaged land after the fall of Jerusalem. When he finally went into exile, it was because he had been carried off forcibly. His own conviction was 'houses and fields and vineyards shall again be bought in this land'.[49] Jeremiah believed prophetically in Yahweh as Lord of History and Israel as his instrument.

Nevertheless, Jeremiah's greatest contribution to the

[49] Jer. 32: 1–44. Cf. especially 32: 15.

unfolding story of the purpose of God was the insight
which he gained into the nature of religion itself. What
is religion? This is a most unbiblical question, in the
sense that no biblical character or writer would ever
pose such an abstract enquiry, and yet it is truly
biblical in that the materials for asking it and for
answering it are strewn richly in scripture.

Is it a means for ensuring that the divine powers of
the universe will be on your side rather than the
enemy's, and will work for you rather than against
you? Mesha king of Moab thought it was, when he
sacrificed his son on the city wall to get divine help
against Israel and Judah; and Jacob similarly thought
so when he made a bargain with the god of Bethel.[50]
Or is it a matter of paying the proper dues to the
proper authorities—'three times a year shall every
male appear before me, and none shall appear empty
handed'? The Ritual Decalogue comes near to teaching that view of religion. Or is it an act of worship,
entering into God's courts with praise and thanksgiving? Or is it a way of life, as the Book of Deuteronomy insisted, in which worship and moral behaviour
both find their place as man's response to the love of
God?[51]

Jeremiah was quite sure that religion did not
primarily depend upon any external object or location or rite. When the ark of the covenant was destroyed, he said it was unnecessary to replace it; when
men put their faith in the Temple, he insisted that the
Temple itself would be destroyed, just as Shiloh had
once been Yahweh's sanctuary and had been burned
by the Philistines; he taught that neither physical

[50] 2 Kings 3: 27; Gen. 28: 20.
[51] Ex. 34: 20–24; Pss. 146–150; Deut. 30: 15–20.

circumcision nor material sacrifice have any religious significance in themselves. But he went further. He recognized that even the strictest rules can be kept to the very last letter, and yet the original purpose of the legislation may be defeated (8: 8).[52] Every corporate institution and every religious order of any age knows only too well that regulations may be fully obeyed and yet the original spirit, enthusiasm, ideal, fade inexorably away. Within a century of the death of Francis, Franciscans were burning Franciscans for heresy; within twenty-five years of Wesley's death, a group claiming to be 'primitive Methodists' broke away from 'T'owd Body' on the ground that the Wesleyans lacked the early evangelical fervour of their founder. In independence of all outward forms, Jeremiah stressed the inner and personal nature of religion.

The remarkable circumstance of Jeremiah's insight is that it followed so hard upon the first attempt in religious history to provide a written code. It is true that the very idea of covenant implies obligations, and that therefore Israel's approach to religion had always been primarily a matter of 'torah'—that is, instruction from the priests based on very short basic codes like the Ritual Decalogue, and guided in developments by case-law. But the Deuteronomic Reformation introduced, probably for the first time, the idea of a written code and with it also for the first time the idea of 'scripture'. It is quite remarkable that almost at once a dissident voice was heard. Jeremiah was probably not totally opposed to sacrifice and ark and Temple as such. It was against a false reliance on these things that he protested. He did not object to circumcision so long as it indicated that submission and dedication

[52] Jer. 3: 16–17; 7: 1–15; 9: 25–26; 6: 20; 7: 22.

which he called 'the circumcision of the heart'. Certainly he did not object to covenant as the thought-form of religion, but he insisted that it must signify an inward and spiritual relationship of man with God. 'This is the covenant which I will make with the house of Israel after those days, says Yahweh; I will put my law within them, and I will write it upon their hearts; and I will be their God, and they shall be my people.' Each man will keep the covenant not by rule or regulation but by instinct and by nature. Thus there will need to be neither law-book nor expositor. 'And no longer shall each man teach his neighbour and each his brother saying "know Yahweh", for they shall all know me, from the least of them to the greatest, says Yahweh' (Jer. 31: 33–34). In place of written code and authoritative scripture, Jeremiah would substitute that personal communion with God to which he had so often testified in his *ṣodh*. For him, that is religion.

If the eighth-century prophets were the first Protestants, then Jeremiah was the first Liberal Protestant. He has all the faults and weaknesses of the liberals in religion—he is unpractical; he preaches a religion to which the common people could never attain; he is an individualist; he does not allow sufficiently for the corporate expression of religion; he makes his own apprehension the sufficient measure of truth. But he also has their splendid virtues. He will not abide cant or hypocrisy; he will gladly recognize truth wherever he meets it; he will follow it bravely wheresoever it leads him; and he refuses to confine it within any authoritative boundaries, not even those of scripture. He recognizes only the authority of God.

THE ANONYMOUS PROPHET

Comfort, comfort my people,
   says your God.
Speak tenderly to Jerusalem
   and cry to her
that her warfare is ended,
   that her iniquity is pardoned,
that she has received from Yahweh's hand
   double for all her sins.

It is now almost universally recognized that at the fortieth chapter in the Book of Isaiah we begin reading the oracles of a prophet other than Isaiah of Jerusalem. Even Monsignor Kissane's excellent commentary, written from the Roman Catholic understanding of the book, recognizes this fact, and a number of conservative Protestant scholars, while in general maintaining traditional views, have to concede the truth of this particular discovery of modern scholarship.

The argument is threefold. The literary style of Chapters 40–55 is uniform and highly characteristic and quite unlike that of the earlier prophet. In place of the short, sharp utterances of Isaiah and his love of assonance, we find long, smooth-flowing periods, often initiated by repeated questions. 'Have you not known? Have you not heard? Has it not been told you from the beginning? Have you not understood from the foundations of the earth?' are the opening phrases of a well-known passage, and its introductory questions can be paralleled many times in these chapters but nowhere else in the Isaiah Anthology.[53] Then again, the content of these chapters clearly relates to the time when Cyrus the Persian is rising to power as world conqueror, that is to the period approximately 555 to 536 B.C. The prophecies come from one living in Babylon among the exiles, and constitute a message of

---

[53] 40: 21. Cf. 40: 12–14, 18, 25–26, 27–28; 41: 2; 46: 5; 49: 24; 50: 1, 10; 51: 12; 53: 1. Rhetorical questions not at the beginning of oracles occur at 48: 6, 11; 49: 15; 50:2, 8; 51: 9.

comfort and reassurance, as the opening oracle declares: 'Comfort, comfort my people, says your God.' It is a promise of restoration after disaster, of return after exile, of rebuilding after Jerusalem's overthrow. Isaiah, on the other hand, lived in Jerusalem during the Assyrian period, a hundred and fifty years earlier and prophesied a coming doom on a city still standing. The third argument relates to the religious teaching. Whereas Isaiah emphasized the moral holiness of Yahweh and his rigorous demands for social righteousness, the oracles of Chapters 40–55 stress his strong affections for Israel, his creative power and his absolute uniqueness. It is not that there is any conflict in the two theological positions, but that the latter transcends the former with an unmistakable maturity. The latter thinker lives in a world of far more distant horizons, both physical and mental.

The Chapters 40–55 are then the work of someone other than Isaiah. But who? We do not know. Living in Babylon as he did, at a time when Cyrus' threat to the Neo-Babylonian empire was growing daily more ominous, and prophesying as he believed he must that Babylon would be conquered by the Persian armies, the prophet no doubt had to remain anonymous in his own day, and he has remained anonymous ever since. He has, to be sure, received a distinguishing label. We have dubbed him 'Second Isaiah' or in a more bastard style 'Deutero-Isaiah'. But his real name is not known, nor is it likely it ever will be known. He is for all time the Anonymous Prophet.

But to know a man's name is often a misleading business. The Hebrews thought that if you knew a man's name, you had a clue to his character, for their names had meaning. Elijah means 'My God is Yahweh' and Isaiah 'Yahweh is salvation'. But did men never belie their names in ancient times? Names today often mean nothing—they are simply euphonious like Janelle, or they have lost the meaning they once had, like Irene. We are asked: 'Who is that man over there? Do you know him?' and we reply: 'Oh yes, I can tell you who he is. He is John Smith.' Because we know that his social label is John Smith, we confidently assert that we know him—when often that and the fact that he is a middle-aged Caucasian male is about all we do know of him.

Since the author of Isaiah 40–55 is anonymous, we are prevented from being content with this kind of superficial knowledge, but since we have the records of the prophet's teachings, we can study them closely and thus come to a truer knowledge of him. We do not know the things which often are the subject of, to use a good old phrase, 'vulgar curiosity', such as his age, his appearance, whether he was married—which matters are his own concern and those of his family and personal acquaintance—but we can know, and are properly concerned to study closely, what he believed about God and His dealings with men. Since this prophet was a creative thinker (which is another way of saying that he was richly inspired) he shaped the thoughts and conditioned the understanding of generations who came after him. Many would say he was the greatest master of language the Hebrews ever produced—a poet to use the conventional term, though the phrase suits him even less than it did Robert Browning. He was also probably their most original and courageous thinker. If we put the two together we can say with some justice that he represents the finest achievement of the Hebrew prophetic movement. To say this is also to say that he is a truly major figure in the history of man's developing thought.

One measure of a man's greatness is the many-sided character of his thinking, or the intimate connexions he has with life at many points. The Hebrew prophets do not normally rank very high when so judged, for they were for the most part men of one burning, dominating conviction. But in the case of the unknown prophet, we are aware as we read his oracles of a wide-ranging interest, which takes him out beyond the usual territory of prophecy. The politics of his day stimulate him, the heroic figure of Cyrus captivates him, the spurious predictive claims of shrine-guilds and their utter inability to substantiate them angers him, while the business techniques of metal-workers, carpenters and potters all provide him with metaphors for his compositions. Nor is he above drawing on ancient myths and legends for allusions to enrich and vitalize his oracles, and the world of nature, its plants, its stars, and its storms are similarly laid under tribute. Even the inner content of his thinking is not dominated by one concept but by several, and in his oracles they appear and reappear, as they are woven one with the other in the unity of his prophetic activity.

How he fulfilled his prophetic rôle is another matter on which we are ignorant. Did he write his oracles down, and were they copied by eager helpers and then secretly distributed as broad-sheets to the various scattered communities of Jewish exiles in Mesopotamia? Were those who took the written word also instructed on the interpretation it should receive, and on its closer application to the political events of their day? Does this explain some of the repetition and the disappearance and recurrence of certain dominant themes, and also does this account for the obscurity and uncertainty of some of the references? Probably most of these suggestions are substantially correct, but certainly our presentation of the prophet's circumstances must make use of creative imagination, with all its attendant dangers, as well as a close knowledge of the political events of the mid-sixth century B.C. Also, we clearly cannot hope in one small sketch to deal with the whole man but must be content to seize on one of the prophet's recurrent ideas, and attempt to trace its development.

When the unknown prophet spoke of Israel's relationship with Yahweh, he continued the best teaching of his predecessors; when he spoke of the rebuilding of Jerusalem, the return of Yahweh to his Temple and the return of the exiles to the homeland, he was dealing masterfully with the best thought of his day; but when he emphasized and re-emphasized the creative and unique being of God, he strode far beyond the understanding of his contemporaries, and laid the foundations of Jewish and Christian theology in the generations to follow. In another aspect of his thought, he was, however, so far beyond the thinking of his contemporaries that after his death his ideas lay dormant in his written oracles and almost wholly unproductive, until stirred into life by the teaching and example of Another, who lived and died in accordance with the Prophet's insights five centuries later. It is this particular theme which we shall try to trace, and in following out the theme, hope to know something of the man.

The name 'servant' as applied to the worshipper of

a god is not limited in the ancient world to the Yahweh cult, but was indeed a favourite designation throughout Mesopotamia, Syria and Palestine. In the great Creation Epic, Marduk, the Babylonian deity specifically stated that man is the servant of the gods: 'Man I will create. He shall be charged with the service of the gods that they may be at ease.'[54] and so we find both the private citizen and the king regularly describing themselves as a god's servants. In the great confession 'to all gods known and unknown', the Akkadian worshipper cries 'Whether he is committing sin or doing good, man does not even know. O my lord, do not cast thy servant down!'[55] and in his prayer to Shamash, the Sun God, an Assyrian king says: 'I am thy servant, Ashurbanipal, the exercising of whose kingship thou didst command in a vision.'[56] A Hittite prayer of the fourteenth century addresses the storm-gods in the name of 'Mursilis, the great king, your servant',[57] and about the same period in the Ugaritic poem 'The Legend of King Keret' we find an example of typical Canaanite parallelism:

> Keret awoke, and lo it was a dream;
> The Servant of El, and lo, it was a fantasy.[58]

Similarly the term 'servant' is used of Moses and particularly of David,[59] as well as occasionally of other outstanding Israelite leaders, and also it is used of himself by the individual Israelite worshipper, who could, for example, say in a thanksgiving psalm:

---

[54] S. H. Hooke, *Babylonian and Assyrian Religion* (London, 1953), p. 67. Cf. *ANET*, p. 68.
[55] Hooke, p. 99.
[56] *ANET*, p. 387. He reigned 668–633 B.C.
[57] *ANET*, p. 394. He reigned *ca.* 1360 B.C.
[58] *ANET*, p. 144.
[59] e.g. Deut. 34: 5; 2 Sam. 7: 5; Ezek. 34: 24; Ps. 78: 70.

'Yahweh, I am thy servant;
I am thy servant, the son of thy handmaid.'
(Ps. 116: 16)

It was also used fairly frequently of the prophets in general, as a class or guild.[60] But it was not used usually of the nation as a whole.[61] For the Unknown Prophet, however, this term more than any other summed up the rôle of Israel in the divine economy; her vocation and election were to the office and task of being God's Servant. Nothing is more characteristic of this prophet, nor more revealing of the man himself than this one fact, that he conceived that Israel was intended primarily to be God's Servant. If we want to know something of the man, we must try to understand his thought on this matter because it is the key to so much else.

Yahweh, he believed, was about to do great things for his people. They were to return from exile to their own land, as the chosen flock of God. In extravagant language the prophet pictures the long journey as a pleasant stroll—a great highway, fully engineered to reduce gradients and avoid wearisome detours, the desert transformed into a luxuriant plain, water always available even on bare heights. It is significant that this is Yahweh's highway, that it is he who is to use it to return to Jerusalem and to take up again his residence among his people, but when he comes he will, like an Eastern shepherd, march at the head of his flock, the returned exiles:

'In the wilderness prepare the way of Yahweh,
make straight in the desert a highway for our God.

---

[60] e.g. Amos 3: 7; Jer. 7: 25.
[61] Cf. Ezek. 28: 25; 37: 25; Jer. 30: 10 and 46: 27–28 are generally held to be later (post-exilic) additions.

> Every valley shall be lifted up,
>> and every mountain and hill be made low;
> the uneven ground shall become level,
>> and the rough places a plain. . . .'
> He will feed his flock like a shepherd,
>> he will gather the lambs in his arms,
> he will carry them in his bosom,
>> and gently lead those that are with young.[62]

Jerusalem is to be rebuilt, and will become a fairy-tale city:

> Yahweh has comforted his people,
>> he has redeemed Jerusalem. . . .
>
> O afflicted one, storm-tossed and not comforted,
>> behold I will set your stones in antimony,
>> and lay your foundations with sapphires.
> I will make your pinnacles of agate, your gates of
>> ruby,
>> and all your wall of precious stones.

The national strength will so revive that Mother Sion will, so far from being childless, find herself playing the part of the Old Woman who lived in the Shoe:

> Sing, O barren one, who did not bear,
>> break forth into singing and cry aloud,
>> you who have not been in travail!
> For the children of the desolate one will be more
>> than the children of her that is married, says Yahweh.
> Enlarge the place of your tent,
>> and let the curtains of your habitation be stretched out;
> hold not back, lengthen your cords, and strengthen your
>> stakes!

[62] The oracles 40: 3–5 and 9–11 though quite distinct have the same theme of Yahweh's return to Jerusalem, and therefore the above verses may be cited together. Similarly, in the next quotation, 52:9 and 54:11 have been cited together. For 'ruby' RSV reads 'carbuncles'.

> For you will spread abroad to the right and to the left,
> and your descendants will possess the nations
> and will people the desolate cities.
>
> (54: 1–3,

This, then, is the theme of 'the Great Reversal'. Now Israel is down, but soon she will be up. Now she is weak, scattered, decimated; soon she will be strong, united and swarming with people. Now Jerusalem is a heap of rubble, a destroyed and literally God-forsaken ruin, but soon it will be rebuilt, beautifully, its bricks laid in cosmetic, its gates and walls bejewelled! Yahweh himself will return to his ancient seat, and with him will come the happy, laughing exiles!

We might well regard this as a classic example of compensation-dreaming, if it were not for two other elements in the prophet's thought. The first is that he believes in a God big enough to actualize his dream. If he had still been thinking of Yahweh in terms of a tribal numen, a territorial, national deity, or even in terms of the incipient monotheism of the Yahwist or of Amos, the dreams he was indulging in would have been merely wishful thinking, quite out of touch with reality. But the unknown prophet had in fact arrived at a concept of God so great as to be the only spiritual reality in the universe. He is the Creator, the Sustainer, the Ruler of all nature. All other so-called gods are figments of imagination, mere nothings. Only Yahweh is Lord. This is emphasized by the prophet time and time again, especially with regard to the astral bodies worshipped by his masters, the apparently all-powerful Babylonian state and its officials. Their so-called gods are, he insists, Yahweh's creatures, and it is he who makes the stars appear, each evening, like soldiers on parade, and because it is Yahweh who commands, not one of them dare be missing:

> To whom then will you compare me,
>> that I should be like him? says the Holy One.
> Lift up your eyes on high and see:
>> who created these?
> He who brings out their host by number,
>> calling them all by name;
> by the greatness of his might,
>> and because he is strong in power
>> not one is missing.[63]

The prophet's vision of the Great Reversal is thus not mere fantasy, unrelated to fact, but rather is grounded on the supreme fact of all reality, the all-controlling, all-initiating power of God. The God whom he worshipped and believed in was indeed One who could, if he so desired, effect this dramatic change in Israel's fortunes. The prophet believed he did so desire, because he intended that Israel should be his servant.

The other element in the prophet's thought related his vision quite firmly to the practical world of men and political affairs. He believed that he had discerned the instrument which Yahweh was going to use to effect the restoration of Israel. The rising power of Persia was led by a man called Cyrus. The prophet was ardently one of his supporters in his attempt to overthrow Croesus of Lydia and Nabonidus of Babylon and so become supreme world-ruler. Cyrus was, the prophet believed, Yahweh's nominee for imperial dominion, and the reason why he was being raised to such a pinnacle of prestige and power was that he would then release the Jewish exiles, who would be permitted,

[63] 40: 25–26. For the military character of the metaphor cf. C. R. North's excellent commentary *Isaiah 40–55*, Torch Commentaries, London, 1952.

indeed encouraged, to return to Palestine and rebuild
Jerusalem:

> Thus says Yahweh, your Redeemer,
>   who formed you from the womb:
> 'I am Yahweh, who made all things,
>   who stretched out the heavens alone,
>   who spread out the earth—Who was with me?—
> who frustrates the omens of liars,
>   and makes fools of diviners;
> who turns wise men back,
>   and makes their knowledge foolish;
> who confirms the word of his servant,
>   and performs the counsel of his messengers;
> who says of Jerusalem: "She shall be inhabited,"
>   and of the cities of Judah: "They shall be built,
>   and I will raise up their ruins";
> who says to the deep: "Be dry,
>   I will dry up your rivers";
> who says of Cyrus: "He is my shepherd,
>   and he shall fulfil all my purpose";
> saying of Jerusalem: "She shall be built,"
>   and of the temple: "Your foundation shall be laid." '
>
> (44: 24–28)

This then is the prophet's vision: the Supreme Lord of
all Being has determined to raise up Cyrus in order that
he should rehabilitate and re-establish Israel, so that
she might fulfil her rôle of being Yahweh's Servant.
That the vision was not wholly nonsensical is proven
by the evidence of history. Cyrus *did* become world-
ruler, he *did* allow the return of the exiles, and he *did*
permit and probably encouraged the rebuilding of
Jerusalem and the Temple. It is true that the fairy-
tale element, the super-highway through a desert-
turned-parkland, the bejewelled walls and battle-
ments, the sudden increase in vigorous population,

all this evaporated in the event, but at least the realities themselves did follow the prophet's vision.

We may wonder how the prophet knew or could be at all confident that if Cyrus succeeded in gaining control of Babylon he would adopt this paternal attitude to the Jewish exiles, and the answer undoubtedly lies in the personality of Cyrus. He was perhaps the first man to understand the potency of well-prepared propaganda, aimed specifically at the audience in view. He told the priesthood of Babylon that if successful he intended, as the Servant of Marduk, to give them back the prestige and power of which Nabonidus had deprived them; his agents also assured various exile groups in Mesopotamia that he would restore them to their homelands and do great things for their mother cities; he projected assiduously the 'public image' of himself as kindly, reasonable and considerate. His efforts paid off handsomely. Everywhere Cyrus had secret supporters, fifth-columnists, partisans and fervent well-wishers. But none was so enthusiastic as the anonymous Hebrew prophet: Cyrus would be irresistible; Cyrus would overcome all opposition; Cyrus would gather the world's wealth; Cyrus would be Yahweh's Messiah!

> Thus says Yahweh to his anointed, to Cyrus,
>   whose right hand I have grasped,
> to subdue nations before him
>   and ungird the loins of kings,
> to open doors before him
>   that gates may not be closed:
> 'I will go before you
>   and level the mountains,
> I will break in pieces the doors of bronze
>   and cut asunder the bars of iron,

> I will give you the treasures of darkness
>   and the hoards in secret places,
> that you may know that it is I, Yahweh,
>   the God of Israel, who call you by your name.
> For the sake of my servant Jacob,
>   and Israel my chosen,
> I call you by your name,
>   I surname you, though you do not know me.'[64]

But for all his fascination with the brilliant, captivating person of Cyrus, the prophet nevertheless sees him primarily as an instrument, the means whereby Israel is to be restored to her rôle as the Servant of Yahweh. The importance for the prophet of this view of Israel as the Servant of Yahweh is well measured by the fact that even Cyrus is wholly subordinated to it.

There is always a streak of hard-headed practicality in a prophet. If this is lacking he is not a prophet, but a dreamer, or at best a poet. The unknown prophet had the most exalted views of Israel's rôle in history, but this did not prevent him from having a most realistic estimate of the dependability and worth of his fellow exiles.

We have to gather from here and from there what he conceived the rôle of Servant to involve, but there can be little doubt that its main implication was two-fold. Israel was to worship Yahweh, perform his rituals, celebrate his name, and accord him that eminence and prestige to which he was entitled, so that all men everywhere would take note and learn what a mighty God Yahweh was. A god without worshippers is a god discredited, a mere *djinn*; but one who is fervently and enthusiastically served by a

---

[64] 45: 1–4. 'Messiah' is Hebrew for 'Anointed'.

prosperous and numerous people is clearly a god to be reckoned with. Though the crude notion that the god was fed by the offerings of the worshippers had long since been transcended,[65] nevertheless the continuance of the cultus, and the enthusiasm and devotion of a strong body of worshippers, were what kept the god alive in the minds of men, and testified to his greatness and power. This 'service' of Yahweh was Israel's primary responsibility:

> I will say to the north, Give up,
>   and to the south, Do not withhold;
> bring my sons from afar
>   and my daughters from the end of the earth,
> every one who is called by my name,
>   whom I created for my glory,
>   whom I formed and made.
>
>   (43: 6–7)

But the other aspect of the Servant rôle was directed out of the Yahweh-Israel relationship into the wider world of the Gentiles. Moses and David had been Yahweh's servants, because they furthered Yahweh's purposes within the nation at large. The prophets were his servants because they spoke on Yahweh's behalf to the generality of the people. If Israel was the Servant of Yahweh it must mean that she too had a task towards others to perform, and this could only mean a mission to the Gentile world. If Yahweh was God of all the earth, his interest and concern could not be limited to Israel only. He must seek the obedience and the well-being of all mankind. Israel then was to be his Ambassador, announcing to all men the truth and might and glory of Yahweh. The word the prophet used was 'witnesses':

[65] The idea is indignantly repudiated in Ps. 50: 9–15.

'You are my witnesses,' says Yahweh,
    'and my servant whom I have chosen,
that you may know and believe me
    and understand that I am He.
Before me no god was formed,
    nor shall there be any after me.
I, I am Yahweh,
    and besides me there is no savior.
I declared and saved and proclaimed,
    when there was no strange god among you;
    and you are my witnesses,' says Yahweh.
                                    (43: 10–12)

The primacy of Israel in the new Commonwealth of mankind was, as we might expect, much to the fore in the prophet's mind, but this should not blind us to the fact that he (and his God) have an unprecedented interest in and a concern for the Gentile world:

Thus says Yahweh:
'The wealth of Egypt and the merchandise of Ethiopia,
    and the Sabeans, men of stature,
shall come over to you and be yours,
    they shall follow you;
    they shall come over in chains and bow down to you.
They will make supplication to you, saying:
    "God is with you only, and there is no other,
    no god besides him.
Truly, thou art a God who hidest thyself,
    O God of Israel, the Savior." ' [66]

That the prophet believes Yahweh to have a concern for all men comes out more clearly in another short passage, of incontestably universal concern:

---

[66] 45: 14–15. I read (against RSV) the last two lines as being still the speech of the Gentiles. Their meaning is 'How could we have been so blind to your presence until now? You hid yourself very well indeed! But now we clearly recognize you as truly the Saviour-God.'

'Turn to me and be saved,
   all the ends of the earth!
For I am God, and there is no other.
By myself I have sworn,
   from my mouth has gone forth in righteousness
   a word that shall not return:
"To me every knee shall bow,
   every tongue shall swear." '

(45: 22–23)

But if this was the twofold rôle of the Servant of Yahweh, the prophet was under no illusion as to Israel's fitness to fulfil it:

Hear, you deaf;
   and look, you blind, that you may see!
Who is blind but my servant,
   or deaf as my messenger whom I send?
Who is blind as my dedicated one,
   or blind as the servant of Yahweh?
He sees many things, but does not observe them:
   his ears are open, but he does not hear.

(42: 18–20)

Indeed, in what is probably the prophet's account of his call to his ministry, he tells us of his deep hesitation to comply, because of his low estimate of the people to whom he is being sent. Only an overwhelming conviction of the irresistible power of God is sufficient to enable him to overcome his fear and reluctance, and to undertake his task.

A voice says: 'Cry!'
   And I said: 'What shall I cry?
All flesh is grass,
   and all its loyalty is like the flower of the field.

The grass withers, the flower fades,
  when the breath of Yahweh blows upon it;
  surely the people is grass'.
'The grass withers, the flower fades;
  but the word of our God will stand for ever.'[67]

It was, then, his absolute conviction of the power of
God which gave him the courage and the hope to
embark upon his ministry; but, while that conviction
never faltered, his estimate of the spiritual insight and
religious maturity of the common people of Israel
declined rather than rose. Israel might indeed fulfil
the first part of the rôle, very well indeed. She would
offer to Yahweh 'the glory due unto his Name', but it
became increasingly clear to the prophet that it was
not she who could fulfil the second part. Yet the task
must indeed be fully and fittingly performed. Who
could be Israel's substitute, to undertake on her
behalf what she herself could not?

If it were not that the evidence is clear and unmistakable, no one would have the foolhardiness to put
forward the answer which the prophet himself arrived
at. Israel was not able to speak to the nations but there
was one who could! Very shortly, Cyrus was to be
world-ruler, and who better than he to speak to all
peoples on Yahweh's behalf? True, Cyrus did not yet
know Yahweh or serve him, but soon he would recognize that it was Yahweh's power which had raised him
up to his supreme position—first to restore Israel to her
homeland and secondly that he might be Yahweh's
Messenger and Servant to all peoples. Cyrus was
indeed Yahweh's Messiah, anointed to this task.

[67] 40: 6–8. In line 4 I have taken *ḥeṣedh* (RSV 'beauty') in its primary sense of
'loyalty'. The last two lines are the reply to his hesitation made by the voice
of inspiration within him: I have therefore differed from RSV in use of quotation marks.

> Thus says Yahweh to his anointed, to Cyrus. . . .
> 'For the sake of my servant Jacob,
>   and Israel my chosen,
> I call you by your name,
>   I surname you, though you do not know me.
> I am Yahweh, and there is no other,
>   besides me there is no God;
>   I gird you, though you do not know me,
> that men may know, from the rising of the sun
>   and from the west, that there is none besides me;
> I am Yahweh, and there is no other.'
>
> (45: 1–6)

In oracle after oracle, sometimes mentioning Cyrus by name, and sometimes leaving the discerning reader— or the messenger by whose delivery the prophet's word reached the original hearers—to supply the name himself, the unknown prophet dilated on the career, the power, and the missionary rôle of Cyrus.[68] The best known passage, however, has been for so long interpreted of 'the Servant'—whoever that may be— without reference to Cyrus that we find it difficult to accept the fact that it was at first—as the detail clearly shows—one of the Cyrus passages, and in many ways the most outspoken of them all:

> Behold my servant, whom I uphold,
>   my chosen, in whom my soul delights;
> I have put my spirit upon him,
>   he will bring forth justice to the nations.

The meteoric career of Cyrus is due to the fact that Yahweh's *ruach* or 'spirit', the divine energy, has been put upon him, so that he may bring justice not to Israel alone but to all peoples! Of course, there are

[68] Cf. 41: 1–4, 25–29; 42: 5–9; 10–13; 44: 24–28; 45: 9–13.

those who think of him as just another candidate for
the office of Gentile oppressor, forever making proclamations of new taxes or military conscriptions, and
there are others who say that one more Gentile overlord and the bruised reed of Israel's strength will break
utterly, and the still flickering flame of life in her will
be put out forever. There are those who have no faith
in Cyrus, those who think he will get so far, but then
he will be distracted or will find the opposition too
strong, or will be overthrown; certainly, they think, he
will never get to the point of controlling Babylon! But
such people are wrong, the prophet declares. Cyrus
will not be oppressive, he will not make the hated
proclamations, nor break Israel's remaining strength
and nor will he fail or be overthrown until he has
world-power and can give justice to all peoples,
everywhere!

> He will not cry or lift up his voice,
>   or make it heard in the street;
> a bruised reed he will not break,
>   and a dimly burning wick he will not quench;
>   he will faithfully bring forth justice.
> He will not fail or be discouraged
>   till he has established justice in the earth;
>   and the coastlands wait for his law.
>
> (42: 1-4)

Such were the prophet's hopes of Cyrus. When he
began to be disillusioned we do not know, but certainly by the time Cyrus captured Babylon in 536 B.C.
the process was complete. At that time Cyrus publicly
announced that he came to Babylon as the Servant of
the god of Babylon, Marduk, and that he came at the
god's call and by the god's power to liberate the city
from the oppressive and unpopular rule of the

Chaldeans. Cyrus very naturally made no mention of Yahweh—it is doubtful if he personally had ever heard the name, though of course his agents had. But the proclamation left the prophet in no doubt that Cyrus was not and never could be Yahweh's Servant.

If not Cyrus, who? After so fearful a disappointment the prophet was probably hesitant to make another identification. And yet, who knew more of these things than he himself? True, he was quite uninfluential and equally unimportant, but Yahweh could soon see to that. He would be Yahweh's secret weapon, and it would be himself, after all, who should reveal the good news to the Gentiles. In a magnificent oracle, he announced himself to the far parts of the earth: he is to be Israel, the Missionary Servant of Yahweh!

> Listen to me, O coastlands,
>   and hearken, you peoples from afar.
> Yahweh called me from the womb,
>   from the body of my mother he named my name.
> He made my mouth like a sharp sword,
>   in the shadow of his hand he hid me;
>   he made me a polished arrow,
>   in his quiver he hid me away.
> And he said to me: 'You are my servant,
>   Israel, in whom I will be glorified.'

He has indeed some of his former doubt, that such a rôle would be anything more than hard labour with little recompense, but he reassures himself with the thought of God's power and His rich ability to reward his faithful ones:

> But I said: 'I have labored in vain,
>   I have spent my strength for nothing and vanity,
>   yet surely my right is with Yahweh,
>   and my recompense with my God.'

His rôle is no longer to be directed to Israel only, or to be confined to winning back to faith in Yahweh all the Jewish exiles scattered in Mesopotamia. He is to be a light to all the nations, that all men may know and share in the salvation of their Creator:

> And now Yahweh says,
>   who formed me from the womb to be his servant,
> to bring Jacob back to him,
>   and that Israel might be gathered to him,
> for I am honored in the eyes of Yahweh,
>   and my God has become my strength—
> he says:
> 'It is too light a thing that you should be my servant
>   to raise up the tribes of Jacob
>   and to restore the preserved of Israel;
> I will give you as a light to the nations,
>   that my salvation may reach to the end of the earth.'
>
> (49: 1–6)

How the prophet expected to become internationally significant and how he thought his words might have universal circulation, we do not know. But if we are inclined to smile at his wild presumptions, we would do well to remember that in sober fact and in ways quite beyond his imagining, his prophecy has more than come true. His words have been studied more closely than those of any other Hebrew prophet, and that not merely in the Fertile Crescent but in the farthest and most distant countries from Australia in the far south to Canada in the far north. There is no major centre of civilization where his oracles have not been read with the most profound attention.

In his own day, however, his ideas must have seemed nonsensical and presumptuous, and immediate success was quite lacking. Indeed his premonition that

his task was not likely either to be easy or to be reward-
ing met with much more ready fulfilment. His dreams
of a new era to be ushered in by Cyrus' success, his
extravagant promises of a new and surpassingly beautiful Jerusalem, his visions of highways running through
transformed deserts were only fulfilled in the most
prosaic and disillusioning manner. It is all very well for
poets to dress their dreams in colourful imagery but
when they are talking politics, people have a way of
taking their words literally. When the new era gave
signs of being very much like the old era, and when the
new Jerusalem very clearly had to be built with bricks
and mortar, sweat and toil, and when Cyrus turned
out to be neither a Messiah nor Yahweh's Servant, but
only a very astute Gentile overlord, the prophet's
fellow-exiles felt they had been duped, and they showed
their anger in rejection and scorn. In following what
he still believed to be his vocation, the prophet met
with hatred and insult and at least the threat of physical violence:

> The Lord Yahweh has given me
>   the tongue of those who are taught,
> that I may know how to sustain with a word
>   him that is weary.
> Morning by morning he wakens,
>   he wakens my ear
>   to hear as those who are taught.
> The Lord Yahweh has opened my ear,
>   and I was not rebellious,
>   I turned not backward.
> I gave my back to the smiters,
>   and my cheeks to those who pulled out the beard;
> I hid not my face
>   from shame and spitting.
>
> (50: 4–9)

The wounds went deep. He tells us that he 'set his face like a flint' and that he relied unflinchingly on the assurance of Yahweh's support and on his eventual vindication, but as a prophet he was finished. Men no longer believed his enthusiastic words, and he could no longer gain a hearing. The well-spring of oracles dried up and he lapsed into obscurity and silence, and what his end was no one knows. He died as anonymously as he had lived.[69]

Before he died, however, he saw one further vision. It lacks the exuberance and the glamour of his earlier pieces, and through it there runs a deep pathos which gains its strength and sincerity from his own wounded and suffering spirit. But out of the travail of his soul (the phrase is his own) there arose into his mind an insight which lifted him above all his political failure and revealed him as one of the truly creative—or since these are two sides of the same coin, let us say in-spired—minds of all human history. The Holy Spirit was profoundly at work in him, using his own thoughts and feelings and sufferings, leading him on to give expression to an idea which was to prove the most powerful and transforming thought ever to have been given to the minds of men. The unknown prophet glimpsed the principle of vicarious, redemptive suf-fering, which when set forth in the fact of Jesus hang-ing on a Roman cross was to transform history and redeem—so far as it has yet been redeemed—the whole family of mankind.

[69] The exposition above takes the more common view that the prophet's oracles are contained wholly within the collection Isaiah 40–55, and also that the pieces are arranged in roughly chronological order. But the New Jerusalem and the Fertile Zion theme largely follow the passage quoted above, and it is possible that (as some have suggested) the prophet was one of the first exiles to return to Palestine, and that he continued his ministry in Jerusalem for at least a short period and that it was then that these themes were prominent.

It is striking that this, the most meaningful of all his poems, has also the most articulate form. Perceptive thought demands from a poet lofty expression and in this poem the structure is an integral part of the content. It begins with a factual delineation of the Servant's ministry. The Servant is to come to great success, but only after an initial period of being scorned and shamed, and the contrast is to be so great that even kings and world-rulers (Cyrus among them!) will be dumbfounded into silence. This is clearly a variation of his earlier Great Reversal themes—the transformed desert, the restored nation, the new Jerusalem—and hardly prepares us for the originality of what is to follow:

> Behold my servant shall prosper,
>> he shall be exalted and lifted up,
>> and shall be very high.
> As many were astonished at him—
>> his appearance was so marred beyond human
>> semblance,
>> and his form beyond that of the sons of men—
> so shall he startle many nations;
>> kings shall shut their mouths because of him;
> for that which has not been told them they shall see,
>> and that which they have not heard they shall
>> understand.[70]

[70] This most profound of all Old Testament passages (Isa. 52: 13–53: 12) poses great problems for the translator. The thought of Jesus and his life and death have inevitably coloured all Christian translations, even to the point of disguising the references to disease under vague terms like 'a man of sorrows'. This with some determination can be corrected. Then, too, the idea of a death and resurrection is so alien to Old Testament thought that scribes have tended consciously or unconsciously to 'correct' and so to corrupt the text to a remarkable extent (see also next note). A number of small but important emendations are fairly obvious, and I have departed from RSV in making them. They can be traced in the major commentaries. But the major problem is whether the vindication has taken place in the poem (i.e., the speakers of 53: 1 have seen the Servant's rehabilitation for themselves) or whether vv. 10–12 are still announcing it as future. If 52: 13–15 is part of the longer poem (as I think it

After this introductory summary, the poem changes its point-of-beholding. We are no longer detached historical observers, but we are plunged suddenly ourselves into the experience of the Servant's ministry. We are those among whom the Servant has worked out the pattern of his destiny, and we are looking back on it all, and trying to grasp its significance. Who while it was happening, we ask, had the insight born of faith to understand what we have heard and seen? Who then could see the hand of God in these strange events? The Servant grew up among us as a very contemptible specimen, one of whom we all thought very little. He was so hit by illness and disease that we kept well away from him, and thoroughly despised him!

> Who believed what we have heard?
>> And to whom did Yahweh's arm reveal itself?
> For he grew up before us like a young plant,
>> and like a root out of dry ground;
> He had no form or comeliness that we should look at him,
>> and no beauty that we should desire him.
> He was despised and forsaken by men,
>> a man of pains and acquainted with sickness,
> and as one from whom men hide their faces
> he was despised and we esteemed him not.

But now we realize that all the time he was bearing this burden of loneliness and ostracism and suffering not because of his own sins, but because of ours! By some strange decree of Yahweh, he has been appointed

is), then something quite stupendous has dumbfounded kings and opened the eyes of the Jewish people to what a remarkable work of God has been going on in their midst, without their knowing it. Only the vindication of the Servant by resurrection seems to me a big enough event to explain the universal amazement. I think therefore that the speakers of 53: 1 have seen the Servant's vindication and that this is the 'observer's view-point' of the poem.

the sin-bearer for us all, and even when we were scorning him most vehemently, he was suffering on our behalf. Because he bore our chastisement, we can go unpunished!

Surely he has borne our sicknesses,
 and suffered our pains;
yet we esteemed him stricken,
 smitten by God and afflicted.
But he was wounded for our transgressions,
 he was bruised for our iniquities;
upon him was the chastisement that made us whole,
 and with his stripes we are healed.
All we like sheep have gone astray;
 we have turned every one to his own way;
and Yahweh has laid on him
 the iniquity of us all.

As we look back on the strange sequence of events, what we remember now is his silence. He bore this burden, and never once broke out in angry rebellion. In massive obedience, with a meekness which required an unfaltering determination to trust in the goodness of God, he played his tragic part to the end, to the day when a corrupt lawcourt condemned him, and they led him out to death and a dishonoured grave. No one then grasped what his lot had been—a destiny of shame and death he had never deserved!

He was oppressed and he was afflicted,
 yet he opened not his mouth;
like a lamb that is led to the slaughter
 and like a sheep that before her shearers is dumb,
 so he opened not his mouth.
By oppressive judgment he was taken away,
 and as for his lot, who considered

that he was cut off out of the land of the living,
>that for the transgression of his people he was smitten
>>to death?
And they made his grave with the wicked,
>and with the lawless in his death,
although he had done no violence,
>and there was no deceit in his mouth.

But his faith in God was not misplaced, and his readiness to further the divine purpose reaped an exceeding great reward. For it was not God's will that he should die thus, unvindicated, unrewarded, unacknowledged. The power and the goodness of Yahweh were shown in that he brought him back from the dead to life again, and gave him honour and wealth, family and friends and the esteem of us all. For now we know that he suffered for our sakes, and that he is our scapegoat, our saviour. He is the one who has brought us into his own obedience and trust in God, and he has become the cynosure of all eyes, the regarded of all peoples!

Yet it was the purpose of Yahweh to heal him!

. . . .
. . . . . . [71]

He shall see his offspring, he shall prolong his days;
the will of Yahweh will prosper in his hand;
>he shall consider the travail of his soul and be satisfied;
by his knowledge shall the righteous one, my servant,
>make many to be accounted righteous;
>for he was bearing their sins.
Therefore I will divide him a portion with the great
>and he shall divide the spoil with the strong;

[71] These two lines are so badly damaged that they cannot be translated with any certainty. Probably they referred originally to the resurrection of the Servant.

> because he poured out his soul to death,
>> and was numbered with the transgressors.
> But he bore the sin of the many,
>> and made intercession for transgressors!

This then is the unknown prophet's final word on the Servant. But who is he? Not Israel, certainly not Cyrus, and surely not even the prophet. His thought has now reached out to an understanding of the Servant's rôle far beyond his own capacity to fulfil in real life. He has come to see that God's business with Israel and through her with all mankind cannot be handled by rulers making laws and establishing constitutions, nor even by prophets giving their admonitions, however profound and true their teachings are. Laws do not of themselves make man good, nor does wisdom teach him to be good. He will obey the law in the letter and break it in spirit; he will know what is right and good, and go off and do the other thing. How shall wilful, foolish, selfish mankind be won to goodness? Only by the mysterious power of one personality to win another to admire, and desire to please, and to enjoy what the beloved enjoys. Let men see one whom they must admire, and who is able to win and hold their affection, and that one loving what is good and noble and true, and they too for his sake will come to despise what is sordid and petty and wicked, and will come to esteem what is good and noble. And once coming to desire what is good for his sake, they will come to love it and to desire it for its own sake. But someone must first win their love by bearing their burdens for them, and in so doing must take upon himself the retribution which wrong-living always brings. When he is seen to have done this, they will surrender their wills to him and be won over by him.

This, the prophet is inspired to glimpse, is the real and only method of making new men out of old. This is the Servant's rôle—and one day, the prophet is convinced, God will send such a Servant into this world. Who, when, and in what manner, the prophet had no way of knowing. He only perceived that when the Servant does come, this would be his task and this the fearful road of vicarious suffering which he must tread. What the prophet never guessed—who could have guessed, until it happened?—was that God would be his own Servant, and bear the sins of mankind himself, within a breaking, human heart, on Calvary. It was because Jesus had read and understood the inspiration of the anonymous prophet that he could say to the two disciples on the road to Emmaus: 'Was it not necessary that the Christ should suffer these things and enter into his glory?' (Luke 24: 26).

Here, then, is one aspect, the most significant aspect, of the teaching of the Unknown Prophet. He is the Hebrew who saw most deeply into the heart of God, and the prophet who came nearest to understanding His purposes. And yet how naïve, how narrowly nationalistic, how disastrously false some of his thinking was! It is a reminder to us that when we speak of the truth of God transcending human wisdom, we are speaking not politely or poetically but quite literally. Even the wisest and the most profound of us holds but a glimpse of truth, treasured alongside many a false notion, many a prejudice, many a downright lie. We have to ask the Holy Spirit continually to give us, as the Pentecoste Collect says, 'a right judgement in all things'—and a deep humility, lest we think our little apprehension of truth is the whole truth, and we become arrogant and dogmatic and deny our neighbour the insight which is his. For all those who seek to understand the business of God with mankind, the words of Job remain true:

> 'Lo, these are but the outskirts of his ways;
> and how small a whisper do we hear of him!
> But the thunder of his power, who can understand?'
>
> (Job 26: 14)

EPILOGUE

As we look over the fourteen sketches now completed, we are aware of the divergent character of the materials with which the scriptures have supplied us. It has been obvious, for example, that some of these materials respond more readily to devotional enquiry than do others.

This may sound a portentous truism. Everybody knows that there is more spiritual food stored in Psalm 51 than in the genealogical lists of Genesis 5. But to dismiss the matter so is to miss the opportunity for some important questions. If scripture is the Word of God, then Genesis 5 will have some significance of some kind, and it may be helpful to enquire: If that significance is not devotional in character, then of what character is it? What kinds of expectancy ought we to bring to different kinds of biblical material? If we pursue these questions, we may arrive at a more reasoned understanding of our own approach to scripture, and also have a more substantial answer than merely to laugh off those who delight in biblical arithmetic, numerology, would-be literalism,[72] and other such aberrations of scripture studies. For it must be admitted that since the loss of the medieval 'four senses', the Protestant approach to the Bible has been largely instinctive, irrational, and confused.[73] It may be that

[72] No fundamentalist is a thoroughgoing literalist. Everybody shies off from the literal interpretation of 'I am the door' or 'I am the vine'. But if we are to be selective literalists, what distinguishes the modernist from the fundamentalist except the degree of interpretation felt to be necessary?

[73] It should be remembered that the 'senses' were developed to meet a very serious need. Already, by the end of the first Christian century, men saw that to take the Old Testament *simpliciter* as the Word of God could be very embar-

a little analysis at this point will indicate in what ways a more profitable approach could be made.

Looking back over the material we have used, we notice a major difference of character between the 'material-of' and the 'material-about'. It stands out clearly, for example, in our treatments of Isaiah and Elijah. Both are prophetic personalities, both are largely concerned with the same problem, and both point toward much the same answer. The two ministries run remarkably parallel on this matter. Yet looking back we see that there is a quite discernible dif-

rassing. It contained trivialities, absurdities and downright immoralities. Marcion's solution was to discard the Old Testament—but in so doing he found he had discarded most of the New as well. Origen, in the third century, faced with the same problem, developed the use of allegory, a practice he had inherited from Jewish predecessors in Alexandria. By means of allegorizing he could get round the difficulties the text presented him with. There was, he taught, a literal meaning of scripture, but there was also a spiritual meaning, the latter being obtainable only by use of this cultured, sophisticated and mature approach to the Bible. Augustine was repelled from Christianity by the thought of the scriptural absurdities he would have to accept, until he heard Ambrose using allegory in his preaching and knew that his objections had been met. By the twelfth century, three senses had been developed, the literal, the spiritual (often called the allegorical and used to elucidate doctrine) and the tropological (i.e. the metaphorical, and used to arrive at the moral teaching). The fourfold scheme is as old at least as the fifth century, but became popular in the thirteenth. It comprised the literal sense, the allegorical, the moral and the anagogical. This last concerned itself with teaching man how to arrive safely in heaven. Nicholas of Lyra is credited with the jingle:

Littera gesta docet, quae credas allegoria,
Moralis quid agas, quo tendas anagogia.

Often the literal sense was brushed aside in the commentator's haste to reach the 'higher' sense of his passage, and it was necessary for the Reformers to place a renewed insistence upon the primacy of the literal sense. Consequently, Protestants generally have repudiated the notion of 'senses', whether three or four or even seven. But this left the original problem of the uneven content of scripture unanswered, until in the second half of the nineteenth century there arose the concept of progressive revelation. This teaching has certainly dealt adequately with the difficulties inherent in the biblical material, but more recently many scholars have felt that it does not provide adequately for the belief that the Bible is itself the inspired record of the divine self-disclosure in history. In other words, it does not provide adequately for just those qualities of scripture for which the old doctrine of the four senses, with all its faults, provided richly. Our problem is to work (as we must) with the concept of progressive revelation and at the same time to make provision for that other dimension in the text, that of inspired scripture.

216

ference in our approach to the two sets of scripture passages, and we need to know the reason why.

The chapters in The Book of Kings which recount for us the stories of Elijah are very definitely 'material-about'. Only one striking phrase impresses the reader as possibly being Elijah's own—'The God before whom I stand'.[74] For the rest, it is all third-person narrative or editorial material. This means that these chapters give us the means whereby we can seriously study a series of third-person beings called Yahweh and Elijah and Israel, as well as the implications of their relationships. From these materials we may deduce or infer suggestive lines of thought which are applicable to ourselves in our own relationships. But when we turn to the Book of Isaiah, we find it rich in passages which are the prophet's own words. By sympathetic identification of ourselves with the prophet, we find ourselves in his situation, and think his thought, and experience his emotions. Our own range of spiritual experience is broadened and deepened by our re-living, in varying degrees of intensity according to our imaginative capacity, the prophet's situation over against the men of his day and the God, whom he was called to serve. This is especially meaningful for the Christian, when the prophet is speaking of his own relationship to God; for then the reader finds that through his study of the prophet's words, he has slipped by sympathy into the prophet's place, and stands himself in the presence of God. God has become a Second Person being. This is particularly true of Jeremiah's psalms and prayers of interlocution with

[74] Cf. 1 Kings 17: 1; 18: 15. It is true that Elisha is also credited with the phrase twice (2 Kings 3: 14; 5: 16) but this is probably by imitation and to underline that he is Elijah's successor.

God, and students of the Bible are often heard to remark that they find Jeremiah 'a more devotional prophet' than Isaiah himself. Similarly, Athanasius away back in the fourth century drew a distinction between the Psalter and other scripture, because, he said, whereas in all other scripture we overheard others speaking, in the psalms we hear ourselves, and find that these words express our own deepest feelings.[75] Probably the reason for the popularity of the Fourth Gospel as compared with the Synoptics in certain pietistic circles is because St. John allows readier identification of the reader with the disciples who experienced the immediate presence of Jesus. We may conclude then that one very considerable circumstance of the devotional approach to the Bible is its remarkable ability to induce within its readers the experience of an 'I–Thou' relationship with God.

It is clear, however, that some passages in scripture do not have this capacity, and that others have it in greatly varying degrees. One of the important preliminary questions we need to ask in Bible study is: 'What kind of religious interest may I rightly expect from this passage?' For to attempt to find the wrong kind of interest in a particular passage leads only to the abuse of scripture. This is the grand error of the aberrationists we previously mentioned.

What other religious interests then may we legitimately look for? Obviously we shall look for theological insights and also for moral guidance.[76] Here we touch on what was to the writer at least the most

---

[75] *St. Athanasius on the Psalms*, trans. by A Religious of C.S.V.M. (Mowbray London, 1949), p. 20.

[76] 'Moral' in this discussion means personal concerns in a broad pattern, and does not simply refer to morality in the strict sense of questions of ethical conduct.

illuminating realization which came during the course of the series of profiles: that when the material is highly charged with the mythological, as is the case of Abraham or Moses, we tend to theologize, and to derive from the study of these men great theological doctrines, such as Election, Covenant, Grace; and that when the historical element dominates, we tend to draw inferences for our own conduct, that is, we moralize. Adam, for example, can only be thought of in terms of theological doctrines—Creation, Sonship, Free-will, Sin—rather than of human situations and reactions, and the same is also true of Noah. But David and Solomon are flesh and blood creatures, and they do not give rise to doctrines, but they do give occasion for serious moral reflection. It is, it seems, history which inculcates morality, and myth which instils theology. Since neither history nor myth exist purely in the Bible (or indeed anywhere else) but only in varying degrees of alloy with each other and with legend, the distinction of the theology or morality which we draw from scripture can never be absolute, but broadly speaking the affinity of theology with myth and of morality with history is a characteristic of bible-study.

The nature of these literary categories is by now well known, but strict definitions are still not easily come by. Myth in Old Testament studies is used for those stories which are aetiological, in that those who relate them feel that they satisfactorily account for some state of affairs with which they are confronted in life; they are universal in that they present either an aspect of the common deity or a common characteristic of all mankind or again a characteristic of Israel as contrasted with the rest of the human race; and they are cultic in that at some stage in their development they were represented in or grew out of religious rituals. Thus the narratives of the Creation, the Flood and the Tower of Babel are ready examples of myth. Probably we should recognize the Abraham cycle as mythological despite its strong element of historically accurate tradition, because the Abraham story has been lifted on to the mythological plane by the strong ideological significance which it has been made to bear by later generations. Similarly, though the Exodus is undoubtedly a memory of some historical event, it too has such a marked ideological significance that the historical has been sublimated into the mythological. Both the Abraham saga and the Exodus saga have, we may suspect, close links with rituals and the cultus.[77] The nature of myth being what it is, the affinity of theology and myth is readily understandable: the theology we now discover in mythological parts of the Old Testament is neither arbitrary nor accidental, but is indeed the original ideology modified and transformed by its place in the unity of the Bible as a whole. Myth, perhaps more than any other part of the Old Testament, witnesses 'from faith to faith'.

History, on the other hand, is and always has been the proving ground of moral principles. Our working definition of history was 'the recounting of past events in such a connected way that their factual character is respected and their significance for the narrator is suggested'.[78] It is important to notice the last phrase. The conscientious historian tells the truth, and nothing but the truth, as far as he can ascertain it, but he

[77] Cf. J. Pedersen, *Israel* III–IV (London, 1940), p. 728; on the relation of the idea of Covenant with the cultus, cf. A. Weiser, *Die Psalmen* (Das Altetestament Deutsch), Third Edition, Gottingen, 1950.
[78] Cf. *supra*, p. 100.

never pretends to tell the whole truth but only his own judicious selection of it. It is at this point that the ideological bias of the historian has greater or less play according to the kind of historian he is—but anyone who reads history, even the history of Rancke, without taking this fact into account is simply an ignoramus.[79] Biblical history never pretends to be unbiased. It is as much the proclamation of a faith as are the oracles of the prophets. But it does this by way of providing a number of object lessons, showing how the great principles enunciated by Deuteronomy and other parts of scripture work out in the actual business of living. Thus the historical narratives lend themselves more often to inferences of a moral character, not in the sense that they are narrowly concerned with an abstract subject called ethics, but rather in the sense that they are broadly concerned with inculcating a particular orientation to the business of living, that is, with what the Old Testament called 'wisdom', 'the fear of the Lord'. When we know the type of biblical material we are dealing with, we have some indication of the kind of expectancy we should bring to it.

There has recently been evidenced a cautious revival of the typological exegesis among some modern Old Testament scholars.[80] We have ourselves argued for a recognition that some parts of scripture respond more readily to a devotional, others to a theological, and others to a moral expectancy, and we seem to be well on the road to reviving the classical 'four senses of scripture'. But two things need to be said. While the literal sense must always be the ground of all exegesis, and therefore the two

[79] Cf. particularly Peter Geyl, *Debates with Historians*, New York, 1958.
[80] Cf. 'The Christian Interpretation of the Psalms', *Canadian Journal of Theology*, Vol. V, No. 1, January, 1959.

schemes may be said to share the same basis, the devotional approach does not coincide with the spiritual sense (which was largely concerned with the mystical nature of the Church), while the moral interest of our own enquiry covers both the moral and the anagogical senses of the classical scheme. But (and this is the second thing) there is a profound difference between the notion of a fourfold sense of scripture and the present recognition that scripture as such can only have one sense—the literal. Anything more than this is not exegesis but eisagesis, that is, not a 'reading-out', but a 'reading-in'. Our present concern is rather to insist that eisagesis as represented by these varied interests of expectancy must be recognized as a proper biblical discipline, and that its methods must be open to analysis and rational procedure—though not to regimentation, since the theological, moral and devotional interests can seldom be sharply segregated. Though eisagesis can never establish more senses of scripture than one, it can distinguish usefully, we maintain, the kinds of expectation which we may properly bring to the reading of scripture.

What, then, of allegory? Is it a legitimate approach in any sense? Some of the greatest preachers of the day still use it with telling effect.[81] But its weaknesses are great, and its temptations are legion. If we take as naïve examples the five smooth stones which David gathered from the brook before he went to meet Goliath, or the four anchors which the sailors of Paul's ship let down during the great storm, we can at once see the ease with which they can be manipulated. We

[81] A good example is Ronald Knox. Cf. *Pastoral Sermons*, ed. Philip Caraman (London, 1960), p. 230, 'The Gleaner', an allegorization of the story of Ruth in terms of the Eucharist; or p. 445 'Mount Carmel' where the mountain is allegorized in terms of Mary the mother of Jesus.

must fight the Giant Irreligion with Prayer, Patience, Penitence, Prudence and Persistence; we must hold fast to our faith in a stormy world by the anchors of Denial, Discipline, Duty and Devotion. Whether we are acrostically-minded or acrostically-allergic, what we make the stones or the anchors represent depends not on scripture but ourselves. The Bible exercises no control over our thought, but is simply the means whereby we express our own notions, whether they be the Platonism of Philo and Origen, or the rotarian values of the social gospeller. Any approach to the Bible whereby we can manipulate it into saying what we want cannot be commended by those who take the notion of scripture seriously. The great appeal of allegory lies in its poetic and pedagogic values, and we shall no doubt always continue in greater or less degree to use this type of eisagesis, but we must at least know what it is that we are doing.

If allegory is suited to one type of scripture material more than another, it surely is that which we describe as legend. Legend is like myth often aetiological, but it lacks the element of universality and is more limited in its scope; it is often tribal—its significance is closely associated with a particular person or historical situation; and it is not primarily associated with the cultus and its rituals. Jacob is an outstanding instance of legend and Samson on a much lower level is another. Legend lies between myth on the one hand and history on the other, but it is not clearly amenable to a distinct approach of its own. It seldom exposes a great theological doctrine, though it often takes cognizance of theological ideas, and once it is recognized as legend it obviously lacks the force of history in inculcating moral considerations. Where it has in the past proved

223

its worth is in its affinity to poetry, probably because of its own initial element of make-believe. Possibly that is why so many of the great legends of the Old Testament have been the inspiration of hymns, from 'The Song of the Three Hebrew Children in the burning, fiery Furnace' which we call the *Benedicite*, to Charles Wesley's 'Wrestling Jacob' or Sarah Adams' 'Nearer my God to Thee' or Philip Doddrige's 'O God of Bethel'. In so far as the Bible is a classic literature, providing Christendom with its fairy-tales and nursery-lore, its poetry and romance, as well as with its stern morality and high doctrine, legend has its own proper place in the rich variety of scripture: 'in many and various ways God spoke of old to our fathers', and He does so still to us.

One last question remains: Why the Bible? Why should it be these particular scriptures to which we come with our devotional, theological and moral expectancy? Are there not other, more Christian writings which would serve our turn better? It is at this point that the historical element in the Bible comes into its own. It is a very respectable element. As archaeologists, linguists and pre-historians have painstakingly reconstructed the history of the ancient world, with a quite astonishing degree of detail, the main Bible story from Abraham to the first century of the Roman Empire has been seen to be solidly built into the historical structure of the Ancient Near East. Every year, more and more evidence links the Bible more and more firmly with the growing volume of knowledge, and the historical element in the Bible is wholly consonant with that knowledge.[82] This is an impressive fact which

[82] Cf. 'History and the Bible', *The Canadian Journal of Theology*, Vol. III, No. 2, April, 1957.

should not be left to the Fundamentalists alone to proclaim. But the important religious conclusion is that the Old Testament is left unique. There is no other rival body of literature which reaches so far back into the beginnings of God's historical revelation. If we believe that we can trace a continuous revelation of God in human history, beginning at least as far back as Abraham, then the book which authentically and contemporaneously tells of those beginnings will inevitably be a basic authority; if there is only one such book it will be a unique authority. The New Testament is similarly unique because of its historical authenticity in telling the story of Jesus, and because there are no rival records. The Christian religion cannot by its very nature be wholly given over to myth, legend, theology and faith—it must be securely rooted in plain historical facts; and in their testimony to those facts, both the Old Testament and the New have been searchingly examined and found to be dependable. As documents they are contemporaneous, authentic, and unique.

Moreover, the scriptures are the possession of the whole Church. St. John Chrysostom means more to the Eastern Church than he does to the West, while Augustine on the other hand has a greater significance for the Western Church. Aquinas means more to Rome than he does to the Protestant churches, while Calvin has more significance for Presbyterians than he has for Methodists. But Isaiah and Paul have meaning for all Christians everywhere. Therefore, while there is no particular kind of inspiration in the Bible which is not to be found in some lesser or greater degree in other Christian works, the Bible stands alone, because it is universal as they are not, and because it is original, whereas all other Christian writings derive from it. We may indeed bring, we ought to bring, a quickened expectancy to the reading of St. Thomas à Kempis or John Bunyan, but historically they have not been and never can become the means of grace which the Bible has proved to be to the whole Church. It is by the sheer facts of history that God has designated this literature as His divine word of self-revealing to all mankind.

Once the Bible is seen to have this historical significance, it becomes reasonable to assume that God, foreseeing the importance it was to assume in the life of the Church, took especial care, if we may use such human language, over its preparation. It was He who inspired the faith that shaped the myths and coloured the legends and gave a bias to the histories, and when we speak of the scripture as written from faith to faith, we have to reckon with the planned and providential activity of the Holy Spirit. We may not so readily as our fathers think of God as 'the Divine Author of Scripture', to use the sonorous eighteenth-century phrase, but we may indeed think in more audio-visual language of the divine Co-author, Director and Producer. There is then every reason why we should still come to this book as to no other with an expectancy that through it God will speak to our hearts in this day as in former days, for it is still what it has always been, the Word of God.

3000 copies
printed from Monotype Baskerville by
Latimer, Trend & Co. Ltd.
Plymouth

INDEX

Old Testament